# The Proverbs 31 Police Wife

Leah Everly

# DEDICATION

This book is dedicated to my husband and son, who have both supported me (and been patient with me) while I've worked on this project, and my daughter who's due in a few months (who I can't wait to meet!). I love you all!

# CONTENTS

# INTRODUCTION

*See what great love the Father has lavished on us, that we should be called children of God! And that is what we are! The reason the world does not know us is that it did not know Him.*
*1 John 3:1*

I've always loved the description of the Proverbs 31 wife. She sounds strong, tenacious, and smart, but also compassionate and kind. She sounds like the kind of woman you'd want to be friends with: someone who genuinely cares about you and really listens when you talk. I can understand why it's such a popular passage of scripture, because she's so inspiring. I can't really think of anyone who wouldn't want to be like her.

The reason I got to thinking about centering a devotional for police wives around this story is probably its most popular line:

"She is clothed with strength and dignity,
   and she laughs without fear of the future." *(NLT)*

As a police wife, I'm guessing this doesn't always describe you, and for pretty solid reasons. Your husband faces danger, every single day. Almost every news outlet exploits stories of officers defending their lives for ratings without regard to how that affects their safety. As a result, he's faced with even more people who hate him for what he does for a living – who see him as a power-hungry tyrant with a badge, not the loving, kind, caring man who you call your soul mate.

The strength and dignity described in this verse are rooted in complete faith in God. For most people, that faith doesn't come naturally. You don't just wake up thinking, "I trust God completely, and I'm not scared of anything." When you look closely at the major traits the Proverbs 31 wife is described as having, you can find a great roadmap for developing the kind of faith that allows you to face the future more confidently, no matter what trials come.

That's the most significant trait I hope this devotional will help you develop, but it's definitely not all. When it comes to being a police wife, your life looks a lot different from that of most of your family and friends. You have so many extra responsibilities and stresses because of your husband's job. No matter how proud you are of your husband, they can get seriously overwhelming. You're constantly wondering whether you're enough: as a wife, as a mom, as an employee, even as a woman in general.

As you work on developing the traits of the Proverbs 31 wife that allow you to live a faith-filled rather than fear-filled life, you'll also find your feelings of overwhelm being reduced. The Proverbs 31 wife is great for all women to strive for, but as a police wife, having something to center you when life is crazy is even more valuable. When godly values like the ones exhibited by the Proverbs 31 wife are your goal, everything else will start to fall into place.

The biggest thing I want you to remember as you go through this devotional is that before you ever became a police wife, you were a daughter of God. He loved you first. He knew you first. He is always and forever your biggest fan. Of all the identities you go by, being a daughter of God is by far the most important one, the one you can take the most comfort in. While you're working toward improving yourself, it's important that you never forget that.

As a daughter of God, you can take comfort in the fact that He loves you more than you can imagine. He's known you since you were in the womb[1]. He knows the number of hairs on your head[2]. He knows the pattern of your fingerprints, the uniqueness of your personality, and every single thought you've ever had. He knows every mistake you've made (or even thought about making) and loves you completely anyway.

Because of that knowledge, you can take a deep breath and relax. There's no need to be stressed out about not being good enough for Him, because He loves you and wants you as you are. As you try to change and improve, remember that He's always got your back. If you're scared because you don't think you're measuring up, don't worry: none of us do. Ultimately, that's not what matters to your Heavenly Father. What matters most is your gradual improvement over time.

Know that God didn't give you weaknesses by accident. Those weaknesses are the very things that lead you back to Him. When you give yourself the grace to make mistakes and learn from them, you can be more sensitive to His promptings and better able to make changes as necessary. Every time you make a mistake, God will be there to help dust you off and get you back on your feet. Promise.

I want you to know that this devotional is designed to be a tool to help you develop better habits over time. It's not written with the intention of making you feel guilty for any flaws or doubts you have. It's designed to help bring you closer to God and live in a more fulfilling way – a way that can allow you to be happier and be a brighter light to those around you, especially your family.

---

[1] *Jeremiah 1:5*
[2] *Luke 12:7*

One note I'd like to make is that I highly recommend you have a pen and journal handy as you go through this devotional. It's easy to forget spiritual promptings in the chaos of everyday life, but if you have a way of recording them, you won't forget them as easily. God will be able to influence you more if you're more attentive to what He has to say to you.

Also, the prayer ideas at the end of each section are suggestions only. This is your spiritual life and your relationship with God. Only you and God know what you need to pray about, and that's why I didn't write out word-for-word prayers for you to copy. I want you to pray intentionally and develop a better relationship with your Heavenly Father, even if the prayer you offer doesn't sound all that pretty. A true relationship with Him is the most beautiful thing you can have.

Most importantly, I want to tell you again: God loves you! Absolutely, perfectly, and forever. Whatever brought you to this devotional, whether it's hardships or just the desire for a better relationship with Christ, I hope it sees you through and that you'll be strengthened by it.

# VIRTUOUS

*A wife of noble character, who can find?*
*She is worth far more than rubies.*
*Proverbs 31:10*

The very first thing that's said about the Proverbs 31 wife is that she has "noble character". Roughly translated, she's a woman of virtue. That sounds great, but what does that mean, exactly?

It's actually pretty simple. Being virtuous means you know what you stand for and you live based on your beliefs. You don't make decisions based on what you're feeling or what's most convenient at the time. It means you always do the right thing, no matter the cost. It means you live with the utmost integrity.

Living in this way means choosing ahead of time what you'll do in a given situation. It means being honest and holding yourself accountable for your actions when you make a mistake. It means willingly taking upon yourself any bad outcomes from your actions, no matter what those look like.

While it's easy to describe, having this kind of integrity requires a lot from you. It requires a lot of confidence, because there are definitely times it's easier to go with the flow, right? It's easier to just go with what everyone else thinks. It's easier to do what they think is best and push your own feelings and opinions aside. Sometimes standing for what you believe in will come with negative consequences – some foreseen, some not. Some fair, some totally not.

Being a woman of virtue means you will always do the right thing even if you could get away with doing the wrong thing – even when the choice is hard. You know that even when nobody's watching, God is always watching (even at those times you wish He'd look the other way, just for a second, so you could take matters into your own hands. Trust me, I get it).

All in all, being virtuous means you live in a way that promotes your values and builds up yourself and those around you.

And as far as being worth more than rubies, that's absolutely the case. My gosh, is that the case! That kind of character isn't something you can buy; and if it was, well, it wouldn't be that kind of character, I guess.

Think about the things you see in your own life. Your husband is constantly running into the worst people the world has to offer. They're people who would do almost anything to make a buck, who could be bought and sold for almost nothing, because they see nothing beyond their needs today – and only theirs. They don't care about the greater good or living according to any moral code. You've got a pretty good grasp on what the opposite of integrity looks like through your husband's job.

Even if not everyone your husband runs into is straight-up evil, it's worth noting the differences between lives led with integrity and those led by what looks most appealing at the time. One of those choices leads to long-term happiness. The other? Dealing with the not-so-nice side of your husband, for one thing, but also long-term unhappiness – a life in which happiness is fleeting and highly dependent on what you have or don't have. One in which joy passes you by, at best – but doesn't linger in the dark times of life.

Knowing what you stand for and always choosing the right thing is invaluable. You can singlehandedly combat a lot of the darkness in the world by doing so. While your husband is out physically fighting evil, you can do your part by choosing to stand with God under all circumstances. You can be a light to the world. You can be an inspiration to others who are nervous about the consequences of their choices. You can make your home a place of peace and rest for your husband, a place where he knows he can depend on truth and righteousness.

It's important to remember the powerful results of living virtuously, because the truth is, it doesn't always feel that powerful. In fact, it can feel like a handicap sometimes. When you see people cheat, lie, and steal and appear to prosper, it can be incredibly frustrating. Sometimes it feels like being honest in this world brings punishment rather than goodness.

What you need to remember is that it's all about the long game. While those who make wrong decisions might prosper short-term, they won't when it comes to the long-term – because they're not choosing to be on God's side. If you're building your treasure in Heaven, it doesn't matter who has more of what right now.

If you can keep that in mind, you'll save yourself a lot of frustration.

All in all, the sections in this chapter are meant to inspire you to be a more virtuous woman, regardless of how hard that can be at times.

# SECTIONS

# VIRTUOUS
## KNOWING WHAT YOU STAND FOR

*The godly walk with integrity;*
*blessed are their children who follow them.*
*Proverbs 20:7 (NLT)*

When your husband was in the police academy, he learned all about the situations he would face on the job and how he'd be expected to respond. He practiced his response to possible scenarios so even when his adrenaline was pumping, his body would respond as it needed to. He was taught to think about every possible outcome to a situation and know ahead of time what he would do if they came to pass.

This is sort of what I think about when I hear the old cliché of, "if you don't stand for something, you'll fall for anything." The reason this style of training for law enforcement is so effective is that it gives you a chance to think through tough situations before you ever have to face them. It means you don't have to go with your gut and hope for the best when stressful situations come up, but that you have a solid, informed plan you're already prepared to put into action.

Even if the situations you face in your life aren't as extreme as those your husband faces, you can still apply this kind of preparation to your own thoughts and actions. Plus, you won't have to go through so many physical defensive tactics or get pepper sprayed – kind of a win!

Having the trait of virtue requires that you know what you stand for and, usually relatedly, how you'll respond to given situations. You have a rough plan for how you'll respond to failure, harmful actions of others, disappointment, or loss. While it's not possible to know everything you'll ever have to face, trying will still put you in a better position when the time comes. Having even an imperfect plan is better than flying by the seat of your pants when life throws you for a loop.

Truthfully, though, life is really good at throwing you for a loop. God doesn't tend to give you things you're ready for, but the things you need – which means a lot of your mental preparation will come down to being rooted in His word, not necessarily having a play-by-play for every single encounter.

For instance, when I was pregnant with my son, we had planned for a home birth. I was so completely confident I was doing the best thing. Even though everyone told me to consider the possibility of transferring to the hospital or even needing a C-section, I thought it such a remote possibility I didn't really do any research or preparation for it.

I was prepared for birth with breathing, counter-pressure, and essential oils, but I was absolutely not prepared for being 23 hours into labor at home and only reaching 4 centimeters dilated. I wasn't prepared to transfer to the hospital and get an epidural, only to have my baby boy's heartbeat fall to 40 beats per minute. I wasn't prepared to be told I needed an emergency C-section.

I wasn't mentally prepared for any of it.

The one thing I had prepared for, though, was trusting God with what He had in mind for the birth of my son. Even though I was terrified as they wheeled me to the operating room, I tried to put all my trust in His promises. I stayed calm until I knew my son was safe and healthy, then I fell into a full-on panic attack because I was suddenly extremely aware of the surgeons stitching me up.

They must have given me some good sedative, because the next thing I remember, I was in the recovery room and they were placing my baby boy on my chest. I cried as I looked at him. I was so in love. The first thing I ever said to him was, "I love you. I would do that again if you needed me to."

Because I had faith in God that entire time and had decided in advance to trust Him no matter what happened, it didn't matter that I hadn't prepared in advance for the specifics of my birth. That difficult experience stands out as one of the most significant spiritual experiences I've ever had, because I was mentally prepared to lean on Him during the hard times.

I planned to trust that He had my back — so even when people later asked me if I was sad I'd had to have a C-section, I could tell them confidently that every minute of that birth made me the mother and woman that I am today. If I'd questioned Him during that time instead, I'm not sure my emotional outcome would have been the same.

Since you can't always foresee the exact situations you'll face, the most important way to ensure you're acting in a way that's consistent with your beliefs is to truly understand what those beliefs are. Fortunately, God has provided a few tools so we can better familiarize ourselves with what He wants from us.

The two most important resources you can use to get to know God better are the Bible and prayer.

The Bible was specifically given to us so that we could get to know Him better[3]. It helps us understand not only what He expects of us, but also what promises He has for us in return. Studying them every day, even if it's only for a few minutes each day, will help you get to know Him better.

One thing I'd like to mention is that even though "verse of the day" apps are useful in their own way, I want to encourage you not to depend on them solely for your scripture study. They're a great accompaniment, but they aren't sufficient by themselves. The inspirational verses on their own don't provide the same context and insight you'll get if you read them for yourself, and won't be nearly as powerful without that deeper understanding.

While you can get to know God through His scriptures, reading them has to be accompanied by prayer if you want a true relationship with Him. As a daughter of God, you have a direct line to Him to learn about who He is, what He wants for you, and what He needs you to do. You can access the most powerful thing in the universe at any moment, for any reason, without anybody's assistance.

As I've grown as a Christian, I've learned more about the incredible power of prayer. It absolutely blows my mind. You can pray about literally anything and everything. God is interested in and concerned about anything you're interested or concerned about, whether that's your work, your relationship with your husband, your hobbies, whether you should buy something or not, everything. He cares so much for you that He'll listen to and provide guidance for even the smallest of problems if you just pray about it.

Add to that the fact that you can do it anytime, anywhere? Crazy. Seriously, even if you can't pray out loud and just pray in your heart, He

---

[3] *2 Timothy 3:16-17*

hears it. You can silently pray for the words to say to a difficult person. You can pray for patience when someone's seriously trying your nerves. You can pray in the car, in your bed, in a crowd, anywhere. I'll stop there before I start sounding like Dr. Seuss, but seriously — doesn't that blow your mind?

If you're ever in a situation where you're not sure what decision to make, pray about it. The more you pray for His guidance and are obedient to it, the more wisdom He'll give you. The more you listen, the more sensitive you'll be to His promptings. The more you repeat this process, the easier it will be to access the greatest power in the universe.

Remember that prayer isn't just for determining what to do, either. Prayer can also be a way to connect with God and make up for your mistakes when you've chosen the wrong decision. You can confess to God that you made a mistake (whether it was big or small) and ask for His help to make things right. Some of the times I've felt closest to God have come as a result of admitting I made a mistake and asking Him to help me fix it.

God loves you so much. He knows you have lots of decisions to make every day, all of which have the capacity to bring you closer to Him or further away. He sent you here knowing you wouldn't be perfect, but has never left you comfortless[4]. Think about it like this: when you watch your kids taking their first steps, do you mock them or get mad when they fall? Or do you celebrate the fact that they tried at all?

As you do your best to understand and make the best decisions in all circumstances, remember that God is your perfect, loving father. Failure can teach you just as well as (if not better than) success, so

---

[4] *John 14:18*

don't be afraid. Walk forward in faith, always seeking His guidance, and you'll be well on your way to living a more virtuous life.

# PRAYER IDEAS

- Thank God for His watchful eye over your life, for His plan, and for His goodness.
- Thank God for His willingness to listen to you, and His ability to help you make the right decisions.
- Ask how to make more time for scripture reading.
- Ask for guidance and peace through reading the scriptures.
- Ask how to pray more purposefully.
- Ask whether there are any mistakes you've overlooked that He needs you to make right.
- Whatever need is most pressing in your life right now, pray for help in making the right decisions, and commit to doing the things He asks you to do.

# VIRTUOUS
# GUARDING YOUR HEART

*Above all else, guard your heart,*
*for everything you do flows from it.*
*Proverbs 4:23*

Confession time: One of my guiltiest pleasures is reading Stephen King novels. He's always been my favorite author — I mean, after I graduated from reading Harry Potter, anyway. I read a ton of them as a teenager, though I ended up taking a break because I ended up getting too scared of them. For instance, I'm still slightly traumatized by *Pet Sematary*. Never again.

A year or two ago, however, I got back into his books when I read one of his more sci-fi and less straight-up horror books. I forgot how much I loved his writing and the way I can disappear into the story. There have been a few of his longer books (I'm talking over a thousand pages) that I finished in under a week — even while working and taking care of a toddler. Seriously, I'm a big fan.

The other day, I went to the library and found one I hadn't read yet that sounded super intriguing. When my husband got home, I excitedly showed it to him and said I couldn't wait to start reading it. When I did, he got kind of a funny look on his face.

"What?" I asked him, understanding the displeasure in his look but not the context.

"Do you mind spacing them out a little?" he asked, "Because you kinda get in a mood whenever you read his books."

He was immediately worried he'd hurt my feelings when I looked confused, but that wasn't it. I wasn't hurt or mad: I was surprised. The effect of the darker books on my spirit wasn't something I'd ever noticed before. The more I mulled it over, though, the more I could kind of understand what he was saying.

While I enjoy those books, I can admit that binge reading them isn't the best for my mental state. As much as I've inherited my husband's ability to compartmentalize a lot of things, there's still a point at which the bombardment of negative images is too much. At some point, they can't be fully filtered out.

When that happens, when my heart is weighed down with those images and my spirit feels darkened, it seriously affects everything. It affects my energy, my connectedness to those I love most, and my ability to positively influence others. And the only reason for it is that I want to enjoy a good book.

As much as I love King's writing, I've had to accept that I can't handle reading everything he's produced. Since this conversation, I've promised myself (and my husband) that I'm willing to put the book down and stop reading if I feel it's too dark. It's hard for me to do, because I'm definitely a "finisher", but when it comes down to it, guarding my heart has to come first.

Whether you share my guilty affinity for Stephen King or not, there are a million things that can impact the state of your heart at any given time. Books, TV shows, and movies are definitely some of them, but then there are also major news stories that hurt to read. There are asinine opinions by people with influence that go viral and make you feel like you're going to boil over. Even lovingly snooping on friends and family through social media can be an exercise in patience and humility.

*Um, YES!*

Many of these things have their advantages. It's awesome that we know what's going on on the other side of the world really fast and can send support accordingly. The fact that we can celebrate the accomplishments of our friends and family through Facebook is awesome. It's great that we don't have to lose contact with people who move far away like we might have in another era. But, as with anything, there are drawbacks, too.

Those lightning-fast news stories, especially when they involve law enforcement, clog up your newsfeed. You're faced with hundreds of inane, ridiculous, and uninformed opinions about how awful your husband and his brothers and sisters in blue are. When you scroll through the comment sections (always a bad idea, even though I do it all the time), you encounter comments from people of all walks of life who you'd never interact with otherwise – which sometimes feels like it's for the best, for sure.

*Story of my week*

Using social media to connect with friends and family can even hurt your relationship with them if you're not careful. It's way too easy to fall into the trap of comparing your own life with theirs. If you're in a good moment, their success might make yours feel not quite that great. If you're in a bad moment, you can start grumbling and getting jealous because, "What did they do to deserve that that I haven't done?"

*Been thinking about the negative affects of social media SO MUCH!*

*probably why I have been so emotional this week.

Everything you do really is impacted by the state of your heart, which is why it's so important to protect it. When something makes your heart troubled, whether it's because of anger, frustration, or sadness, it affects how you interact with others around you, even if they have absolutely nothing to do with why you're feeling that way. It affects how much joy you have when you go through your daily routines, whether those routines are inherently joyful or not.

Most importantly, it affects how well you're able to listen to the promptings of the Holy Ghost. There is so much pain in this world that if you don't protect your heart, it's easy for your mind to get cloudy. It's tough to hear Him if you don't keep your lines of communication clear.

That's not to say you need to avoid everything negative, ever — being cognizant of what evil is and how it affects others is important, because it allows you to recognize evil for what it is. Those negative things can spur you into positive action sometimes, and that's great! What it does mean, though, is that you need to avoid the things that hurt with no redeeming qualities, and to find a way not to dwell on the bad stuff.

The important thing is to pay attention to how your heart is feeling and why. Tend to it regularly, even in the busy-ness of your life, so that it doesn't become overwhelmed. When you wait too long to nurture and protect your heart, it becomes that much harder to heal. Taking the time to heal the small wounds means you don't completely melt down from avoiding those issues.

When your heart is hurting, nurture it through prayer and through caring for yourself, body and soul. Whether that means painting, exercising, reading, journaling, talking to a friend, taking a bath, or whatever else meets your emotional needs, it's worth taking the time to do so. If you make the time to nourish your heart with the things you might consider "non-essentials", you'll be able to do the "absolute essentials" of your everyday life more effectively and with more joy, no matter how mundane they are.

Even if you can only find 5-10 minutes a day for things that nourish your heart, it will be time well spent to be a happier, more put-together version of yourself. That version is the woman you need to be in every area of your life from work, to parenting, to your marriage, to your friendships. When you think about it that way, you can afford to make time for that.

Guarding and nourishing your heart helps you to be more of the woman God wants you to be. Taking care of your emotional well-being in this way allows you to have the energy you need to be the mom, wife, employee, friend, and woman you want to be. All in all, taking the time to care for your mind and soul is going to be worth every minute you spend on it, so don't push it to the wayside. Make it a priority, for your sake and for the sake of everyone around you.

You can't be a light to the world if you don't take the time to recharge once in a while.

# PRAYER IDEAS

- Thank God for the blessings in your life and for His love.
- Thank God for the opportunity to become a better woman through learning how to better guard your heart.
- Ask for help identifying the influences you need to reduce in your life.
- Ask for the strength to take action to protect your heart, even when it's uncomfortable or inconvenient.
- Ask for help identifying the things that nurture your heart.
- Ask for help prioritizing the time you need to care for yourself.

# VIRTUOUS
# WHERE IS YOUR TREASURE?

*For where your treasure is, there your heart will be also.*
*Matthew 6:21*

One of my big resolutions for 2017 was to save $10,000 for a down payment on a house. It was a stretch goal, but I was gung-ho that this was the year I felt was going to make something of myself. This was the year that was going to make up for the crappy year preceding. I *knew* that in 2017, God would make everything right again – that we'd not only get to buy a house, but also have another baby. I was confident that absolutely everything would fall into place by the time January came around again.

We hit the ground running at the beginning of the year. We set aside the majority of our tax return toward the down payment, which meant we were well on our way to meeting the goal of having the down payment saved up before February was over. That meant we still had 10 months to save the rest. I felt so ridiculously confident and so proud of how far we'd come.

In March, however, life took a turn. The weekend after my son's second birthday party, I noticed the water wasn't draining right in our sink. I was annoyed, but figured it would end up being a simple fix. I let our landlord know, and a plumber came out that same day.

Guess what? It wasn't just a simple snake-and-clear kind of plumbing job. Instead, the plumber discovered that the ceramic (ceramic!) pipes in our 100-year-old house had actually collapsed and needed to be replaced – all the way out to the main line. The floor of our home was jackhammered and pulled up all the way from our kitchen, through our main hallway, and into our bathroom.

Needless to say, this wasn't a job that could be done quickly. Our family was living in a hotel for over a month. We were fortunate to have renter's insurance that covered the cost of the hotel stay, but it didn't cover food. Because we didn't have our normal cooking supplies and accommodations, we had to eat out all the time. For the record, we pretty much never eat out because it's so crazy expensive, so this made a huge dent in our normal budget.

On top of that, we also had to spend money doing things outside the hotel room with my son. My husband had work to keep him busy, but I couldn't stay in and watch TV with him all day without going stir-crazy. Sure, there was a playground nearby, but I could only hit it up so many times before I need a change of environment there, too.

During the time that we were hemorrhaging money, I also had drastically less time I could uninterruptedly do my work – which at the time consisted of blogging, doing medical transcription, and taking care of some virtual assistant work for another blogger. I had way more to do than I had time for, and even though my employers were understanding, my time constraints didn't do much for our money matters at all.

I was completely depressed and stressed out at this time. I cried all the time as I watched our hard-earned savings dwindle. I had panic attacks when my son interrupted my work because I wanted to reduce the impact this event had on our house-buying ability. I couldn't believe all my progress was going backwards, and I felt like an absolute failure at life.

By the end of 2017, we were so far from meeting our goal of having a down payment for a house. We'd racked up credit card debt almost to the amount I'd wanted to save for a down payment. That was an extra blow to my ego because I've always prided myself on my financial savviness and never being in debt. It's been my responsibility since we got married to take care of the finances, and I felt like I'd failed not only my personal New Year's resolution, but also my family.

I questioned God a lot during this time. After all, when I prayed about it, I felt like He wanted us to be able to buy a house. It seemed like a worthy goal, right? To own our own house, to have space for our children, to invest our money instead of giving it to someone else for rent?

Somewhere along the line, I finally took the time to think about why that goal was so important to me in the first place. When I thought about it, and when I was completely honest with myself, I realized that I pursued saving for a down payment fervently because I wanted to prove myself worthy to those around me. Buying a house felt like becoming "someone", rather than just a low-level "apartment dweller." It was a matter of pride, of convincing myself I could be successful.

God wasn't being a jerk by putting roadblocks in the way of that goal – even if I sometimes felt that way. When it came down to it, I realized that God wanted to show me that my value has nothing to do with possessions, but that it comes from doing the things He wants for me. When I had pursued that goal so wholeheartedly, it wasn't coming from a place of doing what was best for myself, my family, or for God. It was coming from a place of idolatry.

While idolatry is sometimes thought of as worshipping a golden calf (which, sure, was totally the case way back when), in this case, I was inadvertently worshipping money as a way to prove my worth: to make me happy, to make my family happy, and to do all the things that only God can do. I also felt prideful about being so good with money and that I was better than those who weren't – that I was smarter and deserved more, when the truth is? I was mostly just lucky. God wanted me to know the true root of goodness, and that it wasn't from my own financial prowess.

My heart was not on my treasure in Heaven, but the things I wanted so badly on earth. As painful as that lesson was, I know it was invaluable to helping me become closer to God because I needed my eyes opened to what I was doing wrong. After all, the biggest threat to your spiritual welfare is the sin you don't even realize you're committing.

Idolatry takes many different forms. The world we live in provides endless options for things we can turn into idols – that is, the things we look to which provide meaning and happiness to our lives, to tell us who we are and whether we're worth something or not. These can be things like whether we're smart enough, or sexy enough, or even "police wife" enough. I know you know people who get competitive about that, too.

Even good things can become idols in excess. Whether it's money, body image, weight, hobbies, goals, or anything else, when we endlessly pursue something because we think accomplishing that thing will make us happier, that thing becomes an idol because it takes the place of the thing we should really endlessly pursue: a relationship with God. Without Him, none of those goals matter all that much.

Identities can become idols, as well. When you put a world-given identity over being a daughter of God, you're giving more merit to that thing. Being a disciple of Christ should be the most important part of your identity: more important than your role as a wife, as a mother, even as a police wife. Don't let any of these things make you feel like you're better than anybody else, because that's not how God wants you to think about others. He wants you to support and lift, not condemn.

Most of all, He doesn't want you getting the faulty idea that you're all-knowing, all-powerful, and able to navigate your life all by yourself. Sometimes, He's going to let you fail because He wants you to know He's right there. He wants you to know you've got someone much bigger and more dependable than yourself to lean on, no matter how hard life gets.

If you're careful to make sure your relationship with God comes before all other relationships, goals, and identities in your life, you can avoid the pitfalls of idolatry and ensure a stronger relationship with your Heavenly Father. All in all, that's going to ensure more happiness overall.

# PRAYER IDEAS

- Thank God for the promise that He always wants what's best for you, even when it comes through pain.
- Thank God for helping you identify and fix the things that limit your relationship with Him.
- Ask for help identifying idols in your life.
- Ask for help changing your heart and putting any idols you struggle with into their rightful place.
- Ask for help making your identity in Christ and your relationship with Him your top priority.

# VIRTUOUS
## JUST KEEP MOVING

*Therefore, my dear brothers and sisters, stand firm. Let nothing move you. Always give yourselves fully to the work of the Lord, because you know that your labor in the Lord is not in vain.*
*1 Corinthians 15:58*

When I first moved to Salt Lake a few years ago, I met a woman nearby who had a son about my son's age. She seemed nice enough, so we made a few playdates and got to know each other. My suspicions that she was a super nice person were well-founded, but that didn't change the fact that I was insanely jealous of her life.

See, while we struggled with money, while my husband worked inconsistent shifts and almost never saw our son, let alone had the energy to help with him, she had all the help in the world. Her husband frequently played with her son and watched him so she could get a break. Her mom came to her house twice a week to help her with chores. She fretted about spending money on things that were beyond what I could even imagine, since we were on church welfare at the time.

Seriously, she's a super nice person and we're still good friends – but it doesn't change the fact that, at that time, I felt like the world (and God) were being incredibly unfair. While she seemed to have it all together, I felt like I was drowning under the pressure of everything on my plate.

There were many, many days where my husband left for work before my son woke up for the day and came home after he had already gone to bed. On his days off, he was usually too exhausted to give me much of a break. Our marriage was strained because of his schedule and our budgetary constraints. I was stretched to the limit because I, wanted to be everything my husband and son needed, but also needed time for myself sometimes.

The differences between our worlds was a little hard to take. I'm sure you can relate, though. There are probably people in your life who complain about things you'd kill for, who have no idea how hard your life can be because of the incredible strain law enforcement puts on your whole family.

Honestly, the world can feel really unfair sometimes. We see the people around us get the things we want most. We see doors open for others that seem to be bolted shut for us. We even see people doing the wrong thing and getting rewarded for it anyway, while our quietly good-hearted efforts go completely unnoticed. When that happens, it can be really hard to keep going and doing the things God wants you to do.

It gets even harder when you're facing big hardships, like someone wronging you in a big way. I've heard stories of arrestees specifically targeting the officer who sent them to jail or their families. There are websites out there that claim to encourage transparency in law enforcement, but do so by posting the personal information, including contact information, for local officers.

In a lot of these situations, the wrongdoers still appear to come out ahead, even though what they've done is obviously wrong. When that happens, being on God's side suddenly doesn't feel quite that awesome. Those things can make your faith feel less powerful and more like a handicap.

No matter what trials you personally face, there are a lot of situations in this world that can make you feel like you want to give up. They can make you feel like you don't really want to follow God's plan anymore, because it all seems like too much to take. I want to warn you not to let yourself fall into that trap, because it is absolutely not true.

No matter where you go in this world, you're going to find situations and people who make you question what you're doing and why you're doing it. They'll mock you for the decisions you make, which can make you wonder whether God really has a plan for you or not. Your critics, even your own inner one, are extremely skilled at making you feel insignificant.

What you need to remember is that nothing you do goes unnoticed. Whether you're doing something good or something bad, God sees it all, and, in the long run, will reward you accordingly[5]. No matter how insignificant you might feel about the work you do, you can take courage in the promise that no work you do for the Lord will be lost to Him.

Even if you're not going through big trials in life, this comes into play when you're in the midst of the redundancy of life. Sometimes your list of chores feels never ending – especially laundry, the never-ending story of adulthood. But even that relatively mundane work can be done with an eye single to God, because no matter how small it is,

---

[5] *Hebrews 6:10*

it's important. Washing the dishes means you have clean dishes to eat off of. Washing clothes means you have clean clothes to wear. Every small act of service you do for your family can be done with the glory of God in mind.

No matter where you go in this world, you're going to come across people who seek to move you. To upset you. To make you doubt yourself, your husband, your faith, and your decisions. Some of these people do so with the best of intentions. Some do it out of spite or because they're miserable in their own lives.

Whatever their motivation is, you have to remember that once God has set you on a path, the best thing is to keep on moving. God not only has the best of intentions for you, but also knows everything. That trumps the most well-intentioned advice from people who don't know the plans He has for you.

I know for certain that God sees what you're doing and why. He's interested in you and is always looking out for you. No matter how hard the decisions you have to make can be, know that He sees it all and won't let any good thing you do go completely unrewarded.

These trials are par for the course for the people of God. Even Christ had His critics[6], and He was perfect. Literally, He never did anything to deserve it! If you can keep that in mind and use it to give you strength, the choice of whether or not to follow God is a lot easier to make.

Giving yourself fully to the work of the Lord means doing so in every single moment, not just when it's convenient or easy. Sometimes you've got to drink the bitter cup like Christ did[7] and move

---

[6] *John 15:18*
[7] *Luke 22:42*

forward, knowing He's got your back. The wisest decisions you make will be those based on faith, not fear.

One of my favorite quotes, one I usually see attributed to Mother Theresa, sums this up perfectly:

"People are often unreasonable, irrational, and self-centered.
Forgive them anyway.

If you are kind, people may accuse you of selfish, ulterior motives.
Be kind anyway.

If you are successful, you will win some unfaithful friends and some genuine enemies.
Succeed anyway.

If you are honest and sincere people may deceive you.
Be honest and sincere anyway

What you spend years creating, others could destroy overnight.
Create anyway.

If you find serenity and happiness, some may be jealous.
Be happy anyway.

The good you do today, will often be forgotten.
Do good anyway.

Give the best you have, and it will never be enough.
Give your best anyway.

In the final analysis, it is between you and God. It was never between you and them anyway."

Being merciful and good to others is strength. Be true to what God wants of you, regardless of what other people think, and everything will work out exactly the way it should.

# PRAYER IDEAS

- Thank God for seeing and caring about everything you do.
- Thank God for the comfort that comes from the promise that if you follow Him, things will work out.
- Ask for help making big decisions in the face of criticism.
- Ask Him for the strength to do the things He wants, even when it feels like the world is against you.
- Ask for the eyes to see problems and situations more like He does.

# KIND

*She opens her arms to the poor*
*and extends her hands to the needy.*
*Proverbs 31:20*

The woman described in Proverbs 31 is enormously generous. Even though her own family keeps her busy, this scripture suggests she's always on the lookout for opportunities to help others. I picture her being the type of woman to make an extra loaf of bread for a neighbor who lost his job, or invite a widow for dinner, or be a shoulder to cry on for a woman who's lost her child.

While I consider myself a pretty nice person, I definitely don't feel on par with this standard. I love others and I'm happy to help, but I'm busy enough in my own life. Sometimes when other people ask for my help with something, my immediate reaction is, "Really? Do it yourself."

Honestly, it's not that I don't care about what they're struggling with. It's just hard to fathom taking on yet another responsibility when I'm already waist-deep in problems of my own. When that happens, there are two big things I need to remind myself of.

The first thing is that life isn't just about me. Matthew 10:39 says that if you lose yourself in the service of God, you'll find your life — but if you focus more on preserving your own life than serving others, you'll lose what you're working so hard to preserve. Being a disciple of Christ requires you to look out for the needs of others whenever possible.

Now, I don't think that means you need to serve others to the point that you can barely stand on your own. You definitely need time to breathe and feed your own soul if you want to effectively be there for anybody else. You can't be superwoman with everything on your plate, especially as a police wife. That's emotionally and physically sapping enough.

However, it does mean that when an opportunity to help someone comes up and you groan at the thought, you might want to pray about it first and see whether it's the time to serve or rest. God knows your heart, your timetable, and the needs of those around you. He can weigh all those things and help you make the best decisions. Best of all, even if you feel it's the time to rest instead of serve, He might still help you find something you can do to help – just something a little smaller than they might have asked you for, even if that means outsourcing the request.

That brings me to the second thing I have to remind myself of when I'm feeling reluctant to serve. Being kind doesn't have to be a big, over-the-top act of kindness once in a while. It doesn't necessarily mean flying to a third world country and building a school. It doesn't require donating thousands of dollars to charity. Those are awesome, no doubt, but they're probably not within your reach. That's okay!

In the end, the type of kindness that most changes the world is made up of the everyday, mundane, small acts of love. These are often the acts that hardly make you break a sweat, but moment by moment, have the capacity to change the lives of the people around you for the better.

Some examples of these small acts of kindness:

- Smiling at a stranger.
- Giving someone a compliment.
- Noticing when someone is struggling and giving them an encouraging word.
- Sending someone a quick text about how much you love and appreciate them.
- Choosing not to join in on a gossip session (and maybe even saying something nice about the person in question instead.)

Seriously, none of those things take a lot of effort, but they all have the potential to start a chain of positive events.

The truth is, none of us are in this life by ourselves. Everything we do affects others, even when we don't realize it at the time. Our actions have a ripple effect on the rest of society. The acts of kindness or unkindness you choose to perform, whether they're big or small, impact others in ways greater than you can imagine.

The nasty look you give another driver when they make a mistake could be the thing that breaks them after a week of misery – which is the reason they were so distracted in the first place. The friendly wave and smile indicating you forgive them could help them see the good in the world again when they weren't quite sure they'd ever see it again.

Think about it this way: Have you ever been on the receiving end of a random act of kindness that turned your whole day around? I know I have, many times, but there's one in particular that stands out to me, even to this day.

A few years ago when I was having an absolutely awful time. I was at work, and it was basically a lousy day within a terrible week within a horrendous month. It was the final straw, and I'd gone out to the parking lot to cry my eyes out. I felt hopeless and all alone. I didn't know how I'd be able to physically get up from that spot and move forward with my day.

A lady who had apparently seen me crying on her way in sat down next to me and gave me a fresh bouquet of flowers. She bought it along with her groceries and said she thought I needed it. She listened to me cry and vent for a good 15-20 minutes, gave me her number in case I needed to talk more, gave me a hug, and left.

There are lots of things she could have done instead. She could have walked past and thought, "Poor thing." She could have ignored me completely because I made her uncomfortable. She could have prayed for me, hoping someone else would step in, and that's swell. Instead, she decided to take action and be the hands and ears of God herself.

Can I tell you something? The rest of that day could have gone very differently. I was at my breaking point. I wanted to escape – from everything. I honestly don't know what would have happened that day if she hadn't made the decision to stop and talk to me.

I remember that day vividly, and honestly, I don't even remember her name. But I remember the impact she made on my life. In my journal that day, I referred to her as the angel that saved me. At an emotional crossroads, she walked me down the path I needed and showed me the light.

The life-changing random acts of kindness can be so incredibly small. Seriously, sometimes even a smile or a quick compliment at the right time can have a bigger impact than you could ever know. Of course, the opposite is true, too. Being rude or impatient at the wrong time could impact others in ways you could never have imagined. When in doubt, which would you rather have happen?

You never really know what an impact your decisions can have. Take the time to be kind today, and remember that that your life really isn't about you. One of my favorite quotes is from Albert Pike: "What we do for ourselves dies with us. What we have done for others and the world remains and is immortal."

This chapter is all about how you can be more of a light to the world through your kindness - within the time and abilities you personally have.

# SECTIONS

Love Others As He Loves You
Love Your Enemies
Be Charitable
Build Bridges, Not Walls

# KIND
## LOVE OTHERS AS HE LOVES YOU

*A new command I give you: Love one another.*
*As I have loved you, so you must love one another.*
*John 13:34*

Something that weirds me out a little every time I think about it is the fact that everyone around me has a personal life, a history, desires and fears that are as rich and complex as my own. They all have thoughts, feelings, dreams, secrets, hopes, wins, mistakes — all the same things as me. I mean, maybe not exactly the same, but rooted in a lot of the same things to the point I could empathize pretty well.

My husband experienced this feeling a lot when he worked as a jailer. He would talk to inmates who would say things like, "You don't know what it's like." Maybe "it" was being poor, being homeless, being raised largely without a father in the picture, drug addiction, or something else. Most of the time, he found he actually could relate.

After all, while my husband has never lived on the streets, he has been practically homeless before. He hit such hard times financially that he was living in a camper in someone's backyard. At the time, he could scarcely afford the propane needed to keep it heated.

He understands how easy it would be for someone to get addicted to painkillers because of dealing with his chronic pain. It's why he refuses to take harder stuff now, even though his pain is bad enough he would be totally justified in doing so. He recognized his susceptibility to going down that road and won't take the chance.

His dad was in the Navy and, as a result, was rarely home when he was growing up. He missed birthdays, sports games, and, honestly, most of my husband's childhood. When his dad did finally retire, it wasn't long before his parents got divorced. While he respects his dad for all the sacrifices he made, it wasn't easy to grow up without him.

My husband never talked to inmates in a way that suggested he looked down on them for the mistakes they made. He earned their respect, to the point that he would run into former inmates in our local Walmart and they'd greet him like an old friend. I could never tell whether the people saying "hi" to him were coworkers or ex-inmates.

That's not to say every single inmate was a peach or that they didn't retain a healthy fear of him. He never stepped outside the bounds of a jailer/inmate relationship, but he showed them respect, and that made a big difference.

Hearing his stories when he got home from work made me feel so lucky to marry such a Christlike man. It made me love him that much more. But really, when you consider that everyone has their own lives, that they have a lot of the same hopes, fears, and dreams as anyone else, and *also* that God loves them, too, it's mind-blowing.

He knows everyone's hearts as well as He knows yours, whether they've chosen to follow Him or not. He knows the number of hairs on their head, too. He knows all their deepest, darkest secrets. He knows their grief and shame as well as He knows their joys and successes. He knows what makes them happy and what makes them miserable. He knows their potential. He knows their pitfalls. He knows absolutely everything about them, and loves them just the same.

In the scripture at the beginning of this section, He asks you to love everyone around you like He does. When it comes down to it, that feels like a tall order sometimes. It's not something that comes naturally to me, at all. No matter how nice of a person you are, it probably doesn't come naturally to you, either. It's something that we all have to develop over time.

I didn't know that when I first found Christ. When I decided I wanted to devote my life to Him, I just *knew* that the change in my heart was permanent. From that point on, I was sure I could be 100% understanding of everyone around me. When I went to work the next day, I was a little shocked to discover people still irritated me just as much as they had the day before. Even though my heart had been turned to Christ, it didn't mean my short fuse was gone. I'm still German, after all, and that heritage is not going away anytime soon.

Let's be frank: people can be super annoying sometimes. They do annoying things. They make decisions without thinking about the consequences. They express annoying, stupid, and ill-informed opinions, especially in the comments section on Facebook. As true as this all can be (for me, and for you, *and* for them, let's be honest), God still asks you to love them. Frustrating habits and all.

Talk about a Herculean task. Without having the perfect knowledge that God does, how the heck are you supposed to do that? I mean, even the people I love most can get under my skin sometimes. What about the people who make me want to smack them in the face? Loving others as He loves them can get overwhelming, fast. How are you supposed to do that, exactly?

First of all, I think it's important to remember that every interaction you have with others is an interaction with one of God's other children. Someone He loves as much as He loves you, as unloveable as they might appear before you.

If you keep that in mind, it can significantly change how you treat others. If some jerk cuts you off in traffic, you can react anger and a rude gesture. Totally. But you could also choose to take a deep breath, calm yourself, and think of them as a child of God. If you're really struggling, you can pray to have the eyes to see them as He does.

It can also mean you show respect to everyone around you, regardless of what position they work, regardless of if they deserve it, regardless of everything. You can smile and say "hello", "please", and "thank you" to everyone without breaking a sweat.

Second of all, you can keep in mind that we're all trying our best. Some people have tragedies in their past we can scarcely imagine. Those events have permanently changed the way they relate to the world. They're trying their best with the information they have, whether the decisions they make seem stupid to you or not.

People all have the same basic need to be happy and be loved. Just because someone has sought those things in what you know to be the wrong way doesn't mean they're bad. It might just mean they just didn't know better. That's not to say they're not responsible for what they do – not at all. But if you can keep the perspective that they're doing the best they know how to do, you can take their actions a whole lot less personally.

As frustrating as people can be, remembering that they're trying their best can help you have more compassion for them. It can give you a larger perspective on whatever they've done to harm you (or just annoy you), and help you forgive them more quickly. Being forgiving helps you move on faster and focus on the more important things in your life, so it benefits you, as well.

Lastly, remember to pray about it. While God asks you to love everyone as He does, He also knows you're human. He knows you're not going to be perfect when it comes to this. He knows the length of your fuse. He knows what triggers your strong emotions. He knows you're going to come up short way more than you'll care to admit. The good thing, though, is that He doesn't care about any of that in the long run.

In the end, what God cares most about is that you're making progress. Every time you take the tiniest baby step in the right direction, He's there to celebrate with you, because you've made a deliberate choice to become closer to Him. Every time you make the wrong decision and admit your mistake to Him, wholeheartedly seeking forgiveness and wanting to do better next time, He'll wrap you in His arms. He'll help dust you off and get back on your feet.

As you go through this process of trying and succeeding or trying and failing, you'll come to get to know His love for you better. As you come to understand that better, it becomes easier and easier to love those around you, because you come to understand His unending patience toward you. It can give you the humility needed to occasionally give others a break when they need it.

Loving others as He does is not an easy task. It's not something you're going to learn to do perfectly overnight, even if that's what I expected when I first came to Christ. Remember, that's completely okay! All you need to do is focus on making progress. When you need help, lean into Christ. Ask for the words to say in difficult situations and for the strength to keep your mouth shut when necessary. Admit when you make mistakes and resolve to do better next time.

Most importantly, just keep moving forward! As you do so, God will help you become the person He needs you to be.

# PRAYER IDEAS

- Thank God for His never-ending patience toward you.
- Thank God for loving you, no matter how annoying or hard-headed you can be.
- Thank God for the opportunity to grow and improve to become more like Him.
- Ask for the eyes to see those around you as He sees them — especially those you're most struggling to love.
- Ask to more fully understand His love for you so that you can pay that love forward.

# KIND
# LOVE YOUR ENEMIES

*But I tell you, love your enemies and pray for those who persecute you, that you may be children of your father in heaven.*
*Matthew 5:44-45*

Since I was pregnant, I was part of this online mom group for women who were due in the same month of the same year as me. I loved it! They were my single biggest, most consistent source of support since then. They knew a lot about my struggles as a mom, and I knew theirs. We shared the highs and lows of being new moms and of growing our families. I honestly never thought that would change, because they seemed like such wonderful women.

After three years passed, however, it seemed like things were starting to change. There was more snark, more drama, more taking offense to things that seemed silly to me. I started to get the feeling it wasn't the place for me anymore, but I didn't want to accept that. I loved those ladies, and I didn't want to have to lose that aspect of my relationship with them.

Things came to a head one night when I mentioned how thankful I was when a man at church pulled me aside after a particularly difficult hour with my son. He said I reminded him of his mom, who was a military wife. He said that even though my son challenges me now, he still remembers how much he admired his mom, even when he was doing the same thing to her. He teared up as he told me to keep on going, because no matter how frustrating things got, he was living proof that my efforts won't be for nothing.

That moment meant so much to me that I shared it to the group. I was completely taken aback by the reaction. One of the women said I was insensitive for sharing the comment, because it could be hurtful to military wives. She said my struggles weren't the same at all. It went downhill from there. It went from criticizing what I said, to who I was, to my family, everything. I was eviscerated by a few of the women who I thought I trusted most, and I was completely blindsided by it.

Granted, not everyone in the group was like that, but the ones who were had irrevocably broken my trust. The loss was heartbreaking: almost like a bad breakup, but with, like, 30 people at the same time. I took my son to a friend's house the next morning so I could emotionally recover. That consisted of laying in bed, crying eating a lot of ice cream, and binge-watching stupid shows to try to cheer myself up. I eventually picked myself back up, met with some real-life friends, and moved on with my life.

As with every experience, I didn't come away with only the scars of what happened. I also came away with lessons. While it's not the first time I've been sorely hurt by others, it was another important lesson for me in loving my enemies – which is a topic so difficult and complex it deserves its own section.

We already talked about how frustrating people can be, but sometimes people can be straight-up awful to one another. You see it in your husband's eyes when he comes home and says he doesn't want to talk about his shift. You know it when you see him skip past you and sweep your kids up in a huge hug because he's seen someone else's kids hurt that day. You see it when he climbs straight into bed after work without saying hardly a word to anyone.

As a police wife, you have a more intimate knowledge than the average person of the ugliness of the world. You know some of the worst things your husband has seen (though if he's anything like mine, I'm guessing neither of us know all of them). On top of that, your husband and family are targeted by those who hate you without realizing the extent of what he actually deals with. They criticize you without truly seeing what you have to support him through. Seeing the ugliness of society is hard enough without having to see your husband and his brothers and sisters in blue being villainized.

Seriously, there's no shortage of enemies you can develop as a law enforcement family, criminal and non-criminal alike. Some of them you'll know personally, but others are those in the media who are quick to make a buck on controversial stories or the nameless, faceless internet trolls who apparently have nothing better to do. After a while, dealing with them seems to get easier and harder at the same time: easier because it's not as much of a surprise, but harder because it feels like it will never end.

Tolerating people like this feels like a tall enough order — so how are you supposed to actually feel love for them, no less God-like love? When you're contemplating this question, especially when it comes to the people who have hurt you or your loved ones intentionally, there are a few important things to keep in mind.

First of all, people who hurt others are usually in a lot of pain themselves. People who are truly happy won't ever feel the need to hurt others. People who do rude, obnoxious things or talk bad about you don't do it because they're 100% satisfied with their own lives. They do it because they're miserable and want to spread that misery around. They will do anything to make sure they don't have to feel lousy all by themselves.

Isn't that sad? When I consider things that way and see a jerk not as just a jerk, but as someone who's dealing with a lot of pain, I can suddenly see someone I understand a whole lot better. I see someone worthy of love. I see someone who needs compassion, not more hate. I can have that compassion if I think about how grateful I am to not be hurting so badly I want to hurt others.

It's not always easy to remember that. I'll admit, I'm prone to backsliding and replying with a biting remark when someone goes beyond what my fuse can take. It's a process, trust me. I can say, however, that the experiences I've had of recovering from the injuries inflicted by others' actions have helped grow my patience and understanding toward those who aren't easy to love. The experiences themselves stunk, but God allowed me to go through them for a good reason.

The other thing to remember is that other people's actions reflect on them, not you. Have you ever heard the phrase, "What Susie says about Sally says more about Susie than Sally"? It's true. When people criticize you, it has way more to do with their experiences in life than who you really are.

I can say this for a fact because, honestly, I can recognize this in myself, too. When I think poorly about someone else, it usually has a lot more to do with how I'm feeling and my own insecurities than anything to do with them. When I'm overly critical of other people, it's usually sparked by a problem I'm having in my own life, not because they've done something more deserving of criticism.

When someone hurts you, it's not because there's something inherently wrong with you. It's because they're choosing to be a hurtful person. With that in mind, try not to let it affect your self-esteem too much. The actions of other people are largely independent of your actions.

Conversely, this means that how you choose to react to other people's crappy decisions reflect on you, not them. Being rude to someone makes you rude. It doesn't make them worse, and it doesn't make anything they did go away. I say this after having some less-than-friendly words for people who've hurt me in the past. Being rude didn't make me any happier. It made me feel a little more powerful for about half a second, but not truly happy. Being spiteful is never something that will lead you to happiness — only choosing God's way will do that.

By the way, you might be surprised how far being kind can go in defusing a tough situation with someone. It's hard to continue being nasty to someone who isn't being nasty back to you, no matter how much you might want to spread misery. Your reaction can take all the air out of their tirade. Try it, you'll see what I mean.

All in all, following Christ means choosing to take the high road, no matter what anybody else has done to you. Choosing to do the right thing, no matter what other people are doing, makes you a woman of virtue. Being kind makes you a kind woman. Choosing to do Christlike things makes you more Christlike.

You might choose a course and think you're totally right in doing so. You might feel like you're completely justified in being petty or mean to someone who's hurt you. I get that completely! But know that people will remember the actions you take, not the justification of them. Try to avoid acting on a knee-jerk reaction, no matter how tempting it can get.

It's not easy to be the kind of woman who loves her enemies, but if you can remember how God sees the interaction, it's a lot easier. If you can remember that God will make everything right in the end, you won't feel the need to mete out justice yourself. You will have the freedom to do the things that will bring you happiness, and allow God to worry about the rest.

# PRAYER IDEAS

- Thank God for His willingness to help you become more like Him.
- Thank God for the opportunities you've had in your life to learn how to love your enemies.
- Ask God to see someone who's hurt you with fresh eyes.
- Ask for help forgiving someone else's transgressions.
- Ask for greater patience in dealing with those around you.

# KIND
# BE CHARITABLE

*The King will reply, 'Truly I tell you, whatever you did for one of the least of these brothers and sisters of mine, you did for me.'*
*Matthew 25:40*

When you think of charity, what do you think of? Maybe you think of dropping off old clothes and toys to the Salvation Army. Maybe you think of food drives for the poor or blood drives for the sick. Maybe it makes you think of building schools or hospitals in third world country or serving soup in a soup kitchen.

While these are all great examples of charity, it's a pretty narrow portion of what it actually consists of. These kinds of actions aren't by any means the end-all, be-all of charity work. The truth is, the greatest opportunities to be charitable are all around us, every single day, because we are constantly surrounded by people who could use something from us.

I heard this quote once that got me thinking: "Everyone you meet is fighting a hard battle." I have no idea who originally said it, but the older I get, the more true I realize this is. There are so many things that can go wrong in this world, and it's different for everyone. Some of those things are extreme, like the domestic disputes your husband responds to at work. Sometimes they're so inexpressibly tragic we can't even really talk about them. Some of them are more mundane, like feeling completely burned out emotionally, but they're still hard battles. Nobody escapes this life without them.

Realizing that everyone around you has things that they struggle with means you can recognize that your influence isn't just needed for those in extreme circumstances. It doesn't just mean feeding the hungry or giving money to the poor. You can be highly influential and world-changing right in your own neighborhood through your small, every day good deeds. Heck, with the internet, you can change the world without even leaving your home – for better or for worse!

When you open your eyes to the reality that everyone has hard things they're dealing with, you'll see that there are endless opportunities around you to give someone a little extra TLC. Maybe they have a new baby and you know they could use a meal or two. Maybe there was a death in the family and they could use a friend to talk to for a bit. Maybe someone you know just seems off kilter for some reason and you could drop by a batch of cookies or a bath bomb or something to let them know you care.

This kind of charity is incredibly powerful, and if you don't quite believe that, think about this popular passage from Corinthians 13:4-7:

> "Love is patient and kind. Love is not jealous or boastful or proud or rude. It does not demand its own way. It is not irritable, and it keeps no record of being wronged. It does not rejoice about injustice but rejoices whenever the truth wins out. Love never gives up, never loses faith, is always hopeful, and endures through every circumstance." (NLT)

This is continued in Corinthians 13:13 with, "Three things will last forever—faith, hope, and love—and the greatest of these is love."

Now, I know a lot of people shy away from the King James version of the Bible, and I get it. There's a reason I used other translations for most of the verses you see in this devotional – they're easier to understand at face value. They totally have their place, even though most of my daily scripture reading is done using King James.

That being said, this particular section of the King James version of the Bible has an interesting difference from the other translations I've seen. The KJV doesn't use the word "love" here – it uses the word "charity." It says of faith, hope, and charity, the greatest of these is charity.

That isn't to say each translation is saying something different. That's not true at all. The difference in these translations is that the King James bible is referring to a very specific love: one that requires action. Godly love isn't just about nice words and thinking good thoughts toward others. Truly loving those around you is about taking action to help make their lives better – or, in other words, practicing charity toward them.

When you think about it this way, even the work your husband does every single day is an example of charity. He would willingly lay down his life for the people he's sworn to protect[8], even if they're the ones who also talk bad about him in their personal lives. He leaves your house every day knowing that could be a possibility, but he chooses to take that risk anyway because in his small way, he wants to make the world a better place.

It's important to remember that God rarely answers prayers all on His own. He most often answers prayers through the actions of others. He can help set people in motion to answer the most fervent prayers of our hearts, and if you let Him, He can set you in motion to

---

[8] *John 15:13*

answer the prayers of others. Being obedient is a powerful way of telling Him you're willing to be His hands and feet to change the lives of the people around you.

The work you do is so important to Him that He says whatever nice thing you do for someone else is for them, of course, but He also considers that action as something you've done for Him. That's kind of incredible: that cake you baked for someone who was having a rough time? It's like you baked a cake for Christ, too. Remembering that can help you not burn out so quickly when you're doing nice things for other people.

Because acts of charity are so important to him, it's a great idea to pray about what He wants you to do. One of the most powerful prayers you can offer is to ask to be the answer to someone else's prayer. God can help prompt you to be in the right place at the right time to do so. You can help someone who really needs your help if you have the desire to do so, and He'll be so happy with your willingness to serve others and Him.

Please note that you never know where your prayer is going to lead you, so be attentive to the feelings you get afterward and throughout the day - even if they seem relatively nonsensical. Trust that God has a plan for those who need help, so if you feel really strongly you need to do something for someone, trust your gut and go for it, even if it seems small, insignificant, or silly. Being nice is never wasted.

Teaming up with the Lord in this way is incredibly powerful. It shows Him your willingness to serve, and He will undoubtedly show you someone who needs you. Best of all, answering these small, simple prayers brings you closer to God. You'll be blessed as you serve others with more peace, more happiness, and a better relationship with Him.

Seriously, your charity work doesn't have to be big. You can bake some cookies for a neighbor, buy someone's meal at a restaurant, bring a meal to someone with a new baby, stop and see if you can help someone when their car has broken down (even if it's just through emotional support), or any number of small acts of service people could use. Small actions lead to big changes more often than you might realize.

One important thing to remember about being charitable is to make sure you're doing it for the glory of God, not to be noticed by other people. I love the idea of doing good deeds as secretly as possible, because it helps keep my heart where it needs to be. It reduces both the kudos I get from other people and my desire for it, which helps keep my focus on what God thinks and what those around me need.[9]

Whatever you're doing today, remember that by choosing to perform small acts of kindness, you can make a significant difference in the lives of others, and enrich your world by doing so. Whenever possible, choose to be a light for God in the dark world we live in.

---

[9] *Matthew 6:1-4*

# PRAYER IDEAS

- Thank God for the opportunity to serve Him by serving others.
- Thank Him for the times someone has helped you when you were in need.
- Ask to be led to someone who needs your help today.
- Ask to be sensitive to His promptings.
- Ask for the eyes to see what people need most from you on a regular basis.

# KIND
## BUILD BRIDGES, NOT WALLS

*Blessed are the peacemakers, for they will be called children of God.*
*Matthew 5:9*

If you've been a police wife for any length of time, you've undoubtedly heard references to the above scripture. It's put on a lot of thin blue line-themed home décor, art, and even clothing, because of the whole "peacemaker" thing and its law enforcement connotations. I love it for that, personally. We even have the quote on our wall still because it's given us a lot of strength and inspiration over the years.

Needless to say, you probably easily relate the verse to your husband. My question today, then, is: have you ever taken the time to consider what it means for you?

I got to thinking about this a lot during a particularly rough day with my toddler. It had been a trying week in general, but that day I had finally reached my breaking point. I desperately tracked down a last-minute sitter to watch him so I could have a break (who I think I would have paid literally anything at the time).

I'm a little ashamed to admit how positively gleeful I was as I left the house. My son had been yelling at me all day. The tiniest disappointment caused an epic meltdown. Every time he started crying and whining, I found myself having to close my eyes and collect myself for a second so I didn't yell at him. That didn't work every time, but at least I tried, right? I just couldn't deal with it anymore and the thought of doing something, anything, by myself felt like Christmas come early.

The whole situation made me feel lousy. I was mad because I felt like he was being a disrespectful little punk. I fretted that I was raising a little jerk and I didn't know what to do to make it better. On top of that, the fact that I couldn't fix his behavior was making me feel like a crappy mom. With his constant neediness, I didn't even have time to stop and think about how to make it better. It felt like utter chaos, 24/7.

As soon as I drove away, this story came on the radio. It was ridiculously well-timed, so there had to have been some divine intervention. It was exactly what I needed to hear — and, most likely, what allowed me to go home that evening without needing a stiff drink first.

The message was about Matthew 5:9. I was instantly intrigued because, of course, it's practically *the* law enforcement scripture. I was curious what they had to say. The message was a reminder that as disciples of Christ, we're called to build bridges, not walls, to create peace in the world around us. It related dealing with the unloveable to being a peacemaker, and that definitely resonated with me at that moment.

When I thought about the message, I realized I had been building walls with my son that morning. Because of the week we'd had together, I had spent all that day doing what I could to avoid him. I put on whatever movies he wanted to watch. I encouraged him to play on his tablet. I played on my phone, trying to fake some "alone time" and focus on something lighter than toddler troubles. I tried to get chores done and thought about what work I needed to do later. I constantly checked the clock, wishing time would go faster.

It hit me that at the heart of those behaviors, there was hurt. I wanted to build up emotional walls because I felt offended by his behavior. I felt like he was purposefully trying to make life hard for me. Most of all, I felt like a bad mom. I wanted to keep him at a distance to keep his behavior from affecting me any more than it was.

While it was an understandable reaction, I realized that if I wanted to feel better, I needed to stop reacting that way. I needed to work on building bridges between his heart and mine so we could both get what we needed. My relationship with my son is a lifelong thing, and the only way to improve it is through connection. The choice to love and make peace with him when he wasn't acting in a loveable way was the only possible way to heal us both.

Building bridges with my son meant accepting him as he was − flaws and all. It meant realizing that his issues had very little to do with my skills as a parent and much more to do with the emotional overload that comes with being a toddler. By taking a deep breath and allowing myself to think about things from his position, I could stay calmer and help him through his meltdowns faster.

Putting this plan into action didn't end his behavioral issues. He still threw himself on the ground when I made the critical error of choosing the wrong color cup for his water at lunchtime. The difference in me, though, made for an entirely different situation. When I wasn't impatient with him, when I didn't yell in response to his behavior, when I got on his level and sought his heart, his fits didn't last as long. I was able to help him understand what he was going through, and it meant we connected better afterward.

That connection means he learns from a young age that I'm a safe place to land when life gets hard. Even though his issues right now are small, if he learns at this age that I'm willing and able to help him through it, he'll know I can help him through the bigger stuff later on, too. Deciding to work on being a peacemaker as a parent has changed the entire aura of our household, even if I still have a long way to go before I've got it down perfectly.

This all applies to your marriage, as well. Sometimes when he comes home from work, the simplest question like, "Hey, how was your day?" can invite way more hostility than you expected. I know I'm not the only wife who's been completely caught off guard because I didn't realize he'd had such a terrible day. When it happens, it's easy to respond in kind – because darn it, it hurts!

Conversely, maybe you're the less confrontational type who's more inclined to wall yourself off and give him the silent treatment. I get it, because I've reacted both ways in the past. Both feel safe, but neither one is a super productive solution. Responding either way keeps the hurt going because they build a wall between you and your husband.

Instead of reacting, you can take a deep breath before you respond. No matter how salty your husband is acting, you can choose to be a peacemaker. You can choose to be kind instead. You can defuse the situation before it even starts by either being kind and ignoring it, or politely asking him to rephrase what he just said to you. In either case, building that bridge allows you to really talk to your husband. It sheds light on both of our feelings, which prevents negativity from growing and festering between the two of you.

Changing the script can feel super uncomfortable at first. I get it. I'm not a natural communicator, and the unknown of being vulnerable is scary. I won't lie, when you change things up, your husband might get defensive, mean or otherwise react poorly. That's always a possibility. It could also go much better than you anticipated, though. It could be the start of better communication and a deeper bond.

Actually, those things could happen even if he reacts poorly at first, because at least you're trying.

Just like with my son, you can develop your husband's trust in the fact that no matter what awfulness the world throws at him, you're always there to be a safe place to land, even when he doesn't necessarily deserve it. That's a powerful thing, something he will treasure for years to come. That kind of love can change who he is as a husband, a father, and even an officer forever.

The important thing to remember is that if you never take the risk of building a bridge, your relationships can stall and even whither. As hard as it is to be vulnerable, especially when you're already hurting, doing so will help you find a greater degree of peace in your own life. When you start building the bridge, even if the other person isn't reciprocating initially, you might find your kindness softens their heart and breaks down the walls they've built, too.

Throughout life, you and I both have the opportunity to choose whether we're going to be peacemakers or not. We can choose connecting with others and trying to see things from their side, or we can choose to react emotionally. When you choose to be a peacemaker, you can start a positive chain of events that impacts way more people than you realize. Having compassion on someone can help them be more compassionate to the next person they encounter, and so on and so forth. That's huge.

It's not always an easy choice. Building walls sometimes feels like the safest option when you feel hurt, especially when it comes to those closest to you. It feels safer to keep to yourself than it does to be vulnerable about how you're feeling and risk being hurt any more. However, safer isn't always better.

Remember that when you're doing something God has specifically asked you to do, you don't have to worry that He'll let you down. Your efforts might fail initially. That's okay. When that happens, you can take a deep breath and rely on God's guidance to get through all the unknowns. He'll never leave you comfortless, so have courage, take heart, and take the chance to build a bridge instead of a wall.

# PRAYER IDEAS

- Thank God for every opportunity He gives you to learn to be more of a peacemaker.
- Thank God for His endless patience toward you.
- Ask God for help in paying that patience forward to the people around you.
- Ask for help being a peacemaker in situations you know you have the most difficulty with.
- Ask if there are any walls you've unknowingly built that need to be replaced with bridges.

# PURPOSEFUL

*She watches over the affairs of her household*
*and does not eat the bread of idleness.*
*Proverbs 31:27*

The woman described in Proverbs 31 sounds ridiculously busy. She's a mom and wife, for one thing, which brings with it all the mundane tasks and emotional load you'd expect. She does all of it without our modern conveniences, too – no dishwasher, electric washer and dryer, or anything. She also gets up while it's still night, provides food for her family and servants, buys fields, makes trades, makes coverings for the bed, makes linen garments and sells them, and so on and so forth.

Doesn't that make you kind of exhausted? Just the idea of getting up while it's still night is enough to make me cringe. I have enough trouble getting up when it's light out, to be honest. When you consider all the other stuff – yikes. That's one full plate.

Then again, it doesn't really sound *that* foreign. When your husband is off dealing with his other wife (you know, that whole "rescuing the world" thing), you've got a whole world of responsibilities on your shoulders, too. Even if you work outside the house as well, there's a lot of stuff that falls (unequally) to you.

There's parenting: from the up-all-night newborn stage to the parent-teacher conferences for school age kids to the (what I hear are) incredibly trying teenage years. Most of that ends up on your plate, not his. You also have a lot of the cooking and cleaning responsibilities, lest you subsist on frozen meals and live in a pigsty (no? Just us?)

There's also secretarial work in the form of bill paying and appointment setting for yourself and the rest of your family. There's after school activities, homework, sports, and taking the kids to the appointments you've set. Plus, you probably act as your husband's counselor from time to time and a mediator between fighting kids.

Even if you have the modern-age benefit of an electric washer and dryer, I think the original Proverbs 31 wife could commiserate with your workload. It's a lot to juggle under the best of circumstances, let alone what can be the unpredictable, fear-filled schedule of a law enforcement officer. It's a lot for one person to deal with.

Plus, when you figure in the modern day opportunities for time wasting, like Facebook and Pinterest, you can easily start to feel like you need an extra 6 hours a day, or that you need to stop sleeping so much. It's okay! You don't actually need extra time in the day, even if it would be seriously helpful. All you really need to do is to make sure you're being purposeful with your time. That means a few different things.

For one thing, being purposeful means knowing the most important use of your time at any given moment. This doesn't require you to be naturally type A or have crazy-detailed time blocks in a planner. It just means recognizing the things that are most important and planning your time accordingly.

It also means not frittering away time aimlessly, but trying to use every minute you have to its full advantage – even if it means purposefully taking a nap, because rest is important, too. Living purposefully means you understand the cumulative impact of the small daily decisions you make over time.

Being purposeful also means not waiting until the timing is perfect before you start on what God has asked you to do. It means trusting that any missteps you encounter because you started at an imperfect time are part of His plan for molding you into the woman He wants you to be.

Lastly, being purposeful means using the time you have when things are good to plan for hard times in the future. It means being prepared for things that could come up so they don't completely blindside you. It means using the time you have when things are good to build up stock for when you end up in the inevitable valleys of life.

Your life is a gift. The time you have on earth is appointed by God, and only He knows how much you have left. In that time, He's hoping you'll learn and grow so that when you return to Him, you can be the person He needs you to be. Spending the time He's given you to the best of your ability is one of the best ways to show your gratitude for that opportunity.

The world can offer you a lot of ways to use your time, both wisely and unwisely. Satan does a really good job of distracting people from reaching their full potential, both through straight-up sinful habits and through seemingly innocent diversions. He doesn't want you to do what God wants of you, and he'll do what he can to subvert your course. Don't let that happen.

Spending your time intentionally and prayerfully is part of following God's plan for you. Working with the time you have in the way He most wants you to means that you trust what He has in store. It's a way of expressing to Him that you acknowledge He knows what's best for you and you're willing to do what He asks.

Does that mean you can *never* spend your time doing stupid stuff? No. I'd be a giant hypocrite if I judged you for having games on your phone, because I'm currently slightly addicted to one of those games myself. I'm also no stranger to the occasional Netflix binge. I get it. To be honest, sometimes those stupid diversions give me the mental break I need to get back to work joyfully. It does, however, mean you need to make sure those habits don't take over your life and prevent you from doing the things that matter most.

The main point of this chapter isn't to shame you for making questionable decisions with your time. What I want to do is help you think more intentionally about how you're spending your time and learn to do so in the best way possible. I want to help you develop an understanding of what God wants of you so you can better partner with Him in living your life well.

Because honestly, a life lived to its fullest is the best thanks you could ever give to God.

# SECTIONS

Prioritizing What Matters Most
The Big Impact Of Small Decisions
The Time Is Now
Be Prepared

# PURPOSEFUL
## PRIORITIZING WHAT MATTERS MOST

*Set your minds on things above, not on earthly things.*
*Collossians 3:2*

There's this idea of balance it seems like everyone strives for. People constantly complain about how hard it is to balance work, motherhood, personal time, time as a couple, exercise time, and so on. There's this super ideal image of doing a little of everything, every single day, where you're completely, totally balanced with your time.

Can I tell you something important? That ideal is a myth.

I wish I'd known that when I first got married. I wanted to do it all, thinking everyone else who said marriage was hard was just doing it wrong. I wanted to be Super Wife — that wife who had it all together. The one who stayed fit and pretty, even after kids. The one who worked and brought in money, but still kept the house nice and clean. I also wanted to pursue my hobbies and interests so I never lost my sense of "self" in marriage. I was also very into unprocessed food and "clean eating".

Needless to say, that didn't work out. Over time, I had to realize that the reason nobody around me could do all those things at the same time is because it's just not possible. We all have to make choices with our time about what's most important, and that often means there can't be any ties. I had to let go of the things I thought were so important in favor of the things that actually were.

For instance, I thought it was extremely important to eat only organic, unprocessed foods. I still think it's a nice idea, but our budget hasn't matched that ideal in years. I could either choose to be fed 50% of the time with great food, or do my best within my abilities and eat 100% of the time. I'll choose the latter any day, even if five-years-ago me would cringe at the fact I had chips and queso for dinner tonight (true story).

Each day only allows for so much time to do things, no matter how great our intentions are. Our best laid plans go awry a lot by virtue of kids getting sick, husbands getting called in unexpectedly, or any number of "surprises" that come your way. You can't have everything at once, and that's okay. It doesn't mean there's anything wrong with you! It just means you're wonderfully human and have the same limits as everyone else.

Sometimes your marriage will be going amazingly well, but you're a little less in tune with your kids. Sometimes you're killing it at work, but letting more things slide at home. Maybe you've just gotten into a fun new hobby, and it's pretty much taken up all your time while your house falls into shambles. I've been there, done that, and it's totally okay.

Remember that we all go through different seasons in life where some things take precedence over others, and sometimes what takes precedence one week isn't what takes precedence the next. We operate in surges most of the time. If you can learn to accept that instead of fighting it, you can move on to the next step: using your time intentionally.

Instead of obsessing about balance all the time and trying to do a little of everything each day, think about making conscious decisions about how you're using your time. That means you need to prioritize what the most important thing is at any given time, and what trades you're willing to make to make that happen. Instead of balance, you have to make trades to make time for what matters most.

When you're deciding what time trades to make, consider what makes you happiest. For instance, maybe it's most important to you to have a tidy house – and maybe a spotless, Martha Stewart-worthy house just isn't in the cards in your stage of life. As the mom of a toddler, I can relate. Instead of worrying about what you can't do, though, you can ask yourself: when it comes to a clean house, what's most important? Do you go nuts if your sink is full of dishes? Do you have trouble sleeping if your bedroom is cluttered? Whatever that thing is, make *that* your priority and let the little things go for the most part.

While you can still plan a solid deep clean once in a while, you can own the decision to make those big things a priority over scrubbing the wall tiles in the bathroom once a week, even though they don't really get that dirty. If you didn't catch it, that's me speaking from experience here.

What matters most is going to be different for every person. Take note of what matters most to you and your husband, and let the rest go. You don't need to clean stuff that's not dirty in the name of being The Best Housekeeper In The World. Frankly, God doesn't really care if you acquire that title. He wants you to do the things that matter, and I think that's why He gives us the limited time He gives us: so that we can learn that prioritization.

It can take time to figure out what's truly most important to you. It's especially tough when you're married, because you have two sets of expectations and desires to combine. Whether it's that your husband likes the kitchen clean but you're more inclined toward a clean bathroom, or being accepting of each other's de-stressing regimens, it's one of the toughest things about marriage. Do your best to communicate about what's most important to both of you and focus on giving each other grace when needed.

What can take even longer, though, is learning to make peace with what you can't do. It's hard to admit you can't do it all, especially when you're a perfectionist like I can be. It takes a healthy dose of humility to admit that even if you want something to be important to you, it's just not a priority for you at the moment. As someone with a drawer full of Beachbody t-shirts who doesn't have the energy to work out at the moment, I can tell you I completely get it.

The one constant to remember when you're making your time trades is that what matters most is what lasts the longest — meaning, your marriage and your family need to consistently be at the top of your list. Sometimes it's okay for your to-do list around the house to be neglected so you can be totally in tune with your family. You can take time to care for your own mental well-being instead of checking off stuff on your to-do list. It's all an investment in what matters most in the long run.

I know it's hard to accept that you can't do it all. Believe me when I say I get as stressed out as the next person when I think of all the things I'd like to do in a given day and realize it's not possible. If you can make peace with the fact that you have to choose what's most important, you can feel more at peace about letting the rest slide.

Knowing why you're choosing a particular thing at a particular time can allow you to feel less guilty about the things you weren't able to get done, because you know what the trade-off was. You can take comfort in the fact that you chose something that was more important to you. You can know that it wasn't wasted time, but an intentional trade for your time.

When you focus less on trying to do it all and more on your next best thing, your life will absolutely change for the better. You'll feel more accomplished. The things that matter will get done. Best of all, you'll allow God more room in your life to help you work on the things that matter most to Him. That's worth all the trades in the world.

# PRAYER IDEAS

- Thank God for the time He's allowed you to have on earth and the life He's given you.
- Thank God for understanding your limits as a mortal being, and ask for help giving yourself the same grace.
- Ask for help identifying over-the-top time-wasters in your life.
- Ask for help reducing their influence.
- If you're feeling overwhelmed, ask God which of your goals are most important to Him.
- Ask Him to guide you to the things He most wants you to do.
- Ask for peace in letting the things that don't matter as much go.

# PURPOSEFUL
# SMALL DECISIONS HAVE A BIG IMPACT

*The soul of the sluggard craves and gets nothing,*
*while the soul of the diligent is richly supplied.*
*Proverbs 13:4*

I've always been very much an "instant gratification" person. I can't tell you the number of things I quit as a child and young adult because I wasn't an immediate savant at it. I had the misguided idea that if you were supposed to do something, you'd just naturally be good at it. I didn't understand the necessary process of being a beginner and progressing until you became good at it. With that mindset, I was understandably quick to lose confidence when I tried new things.

Fortunately, God has given me lots of opportunities to learn that lesson. The best example is actually how you probably got to know my writing in the first place: blogging. When I first started my blog, I didn't have that long every day to work on it. I knew it was something God wanted me to do, and I was so excited. I felt like I could be in the realm of "overnight success story" with God on my side, especially because I personally knew someone who had been practically an overnight success. I was super confident I could do the same.

Needless to say, God had other plans in mind. I felt frustrated at first, but I've come to realize that blogging is the first time I've ever understood the value of slow growth. It's the first time I've allowed myself to grow and get better over time without giving up prematurely. Trust me when I say I'm a much better writer than I was when I first started (and no, I won't show you those old posts to prove it). He wanted to teach me patience and the value of working toward a goal for a long time before it comes to fruition.

More than anything, He wanted to show me the importance of being diligent. Nothing I've accomplished in the last three years has come from a place of comfort. All those awesome things have come from the decision to consistently work on what He called me to do, even when it wasn't the most convenient or when I felt afraid to move forward.

If He'd granted me that overnight success, I would never have learned how our small decisions add up to the things we want most. When I saw that, I also began to value the small lessons I learned in other areas of life, like the opportunity God gave me to learn how to cope with jealousy over a female partner when I was introduced to one of my husband's stunningly gorgeous fellow trainees.

That jealousy didn't disappear overnight. The days my husband was gone for training were incredibly long – for a number of reasons – and that insecurity was hard to cope with. Over time, as I made decisions that led me closer to who I wanted to be (a non-jealous, confident partner to my husband), I learned lots of valuable lessons. That maturity couldn't have developed overnight, and if it had, it would have been far less impactful on my journey in being married to my husband.

The value of slow progress is also something we need to remember when it comes to God[10]. Developing an understanding of God isn't an overnight process, either. It's something that requires small, intentional efforts over time as we gradually learn about Him, step by step. Every day, little by little, we can choose to come closer to Him or move further away.

I've heard of our individual relationships with God being compared to moving up a downward-running escalator. Without constant motion, the world is really good at pulling us down. Following Him requires that we keep taking steps in the direction He asks us to. If we don't, our faith wanes and our testimonies dwindle until, eventually, we question whether we ever believed what we said we believed.

The great thing, though, is that He doesn't actually ask that much of us on the surface. As you take those baby steps deeper into the relationship with Him, He'll ask more, but it's okay to go through seasons of spiritual maintenance versus growth. That might be because you've never experienced God before. It could be because you're in a busy season of life and barely have time to breathe, so you don't necessarily have the calm one-on-one time with Him that you might have had before.

Regardless, He doesn't expect you to be perfect day in and day out. All He asks is that you keep moving. Even if the only step forward you can make is praying a quick prayer before you pass out from exhaustion, that's still a conscious decision you've made to do something to nurture your relationship with Him. That's still significant.

I don't think I'm alone in enjoying quick wins and fast progress. I think it's a pretty human thing to want instant gratification, whether it's starting and finishing a project in one sitting or Googling a question

---

[10] *Zechariah 4:10*

and getting an immediate answer. Unfortunately, that's usually not God's way of doing things.

Most things in life require us to slowly grow and develop over time, kind of like a caterpillar turning into a butterfly. We have to go through the stages of growth, the awkward stages of waiting for our wings to grow, and the eventual end result of being perfectly formed into a butterfly. Unfortunately for us, we don't have the same rough timeline and linear stages, but our growth as children of God is kind of the same.

Everything you want starts like that tiny caterpillar[11]. It has to be fed and nourished over time, but honestly, for a while, it still looks like a caterpillar, just a little bigger. Every now and then, you'll have to shed your skin to get a little closer to your eventual goals. Unfortunately, even then, you'll still look pretty much like a caterpillar, just maybe with a few added spikes or colors. Getting through that "messy middle" stage takes a lot of faith, but if you understand that as a natural stage of development, it's easier to keep pushing forward.

Then, of course, you reach the chrysalis stage. You're seeing some progress, but gosh — it doesn't look like the progress you expected. You feel like something's happening and that God is working stuff in your favor, but you can't quite see the progress. You just look kind of like a dead leaf. Again, you need to keep up the faith to move through without giving up.

These aren't the nicest stages, but they're essential. When we eventually emerge from this stage of uncertainty, we come out nothing like we were before. We're better. We've shed the stuff we didn't need and grew the stuff we did need. We've become more like what God wants us to be. The only way that change was possible was through our small, consistent efforts over time.

---

[11] *Mark 4:26-29*

These stages don't just apply to your faith, which is truly a life-long pursuit. They apply to everything you seek to accomplish in your life, whether we're talking about is personal development, like becoming more optimistic, losing a little extra weight, or improving our relationships with others. All those things depend on the small daily decisions we make that can either feed or starve our long-term progress.

Don't give up on the things God has called you to do just because your progress appears to have stalled. If what you're pursuing is something you've prayed about and feel good about, keep going. Having faith in God's plan means pushing through the lulls of zero visible growth and continuing to plug away, trusting that He knows what's best for you.

I know your husband's schedule is crazy. I know you feel lonely. I know you struggle when you feel like a married single mom. All those things are enough to make you want to sacrifice the goals you hold most dearly in your heart, and I get it. I want to encourage you to keep holding on and taking whatever baby steps you can. If you do, you can and will get where you want to be.

Maybe that means waking up a little earlier to pursue your personal goals like writing a book, getting in shape, or learning a new hobby. Maybe it means saying a quick prayer before you respond to a grumpy husband or child. Maybe it means accepting that even if you get to church a little late, being there for any of the service is worth showing God He's worth making time for.

The question you need to ask yourself is, where do you want to be in a few weeks, or months, or years? You might think about that for just a moment, or you might consider actually writing down a list. That's up to you, though I'm an avid list writer, so I definitely recommend that. You can even type it out as a note in your phone. Whatever works best for you, really.

If you're not sure about what to do or what decision to make, remember that you can always pray about it. God wants to help and He'll always be there for you, even if what you're asking seems kind of silly to you. Don't ever forget that what's important to you is important to Him.

The most important thing is that you don't give up, no matter how slow your progress feels. Slow progress is still forward progress. Know that He wants you to do it for a reason, and that He only intends good things for you. Even setbacks can be for your good. Keep taking steps forward, even if it's only a little bit at a time, and know that you'll eventually get to where He wants you to be.

# PRAYER IDEAS

- Thank God for doing small things in your life to lead you to His eventual grand plan for you.
- Thank God for the assurance that even when you feel like your life is at a standstill, He is still working things for your good.
- Ask for help clarifying your goals in life to align with what He wants for you.
- Ask for encouragement when the going gets rough.
- When you're struggling to find the baby steps to bring you closer to your goals, ask Him for help knowing what you should do.

# PURPOSEFUL
# THE TIME IS NOW

*Farmers who wait for perfect weather never plant.*
*If they watch every cloud, they never harvest.*
*Ecclesiastes 11:4*

While I'm usually very much a get-up-and-go kind of person, the procrastination bug still bites me more than I'd like to admit. Whether it's because I'm intimidated, overwhelmed, or I just don't want to do that thing, I can be a pro at putting things off if I don't feel like doing them.

Heck, while editing this very devotional, I spent a few days working on a just-for-fun fiction book that I convinced myself was of the utmost importance. Sometimes editing blog posts drives me to clean the entire house because I'm just not in the mood. Call me the productive procrastinator, if you will.

It's not that I don't care about the things I procrastinate on. It usually has way more to do with the fact that I'm feeling overwhelmed (as was the case with this devotional) or the fact that I'm physically exhausted (like editing blog posts and being 5 months pregnant – it happens!)

Regardless of the reason, I recognize it's a bad habit. Fortunately, I know I'm in pretty good company. You might be reading this and laughing to yourself (or cringing) because you do the same thing. It's natural to put things off because they seem too hard — whether it's because we really, really want them, or because they don't seem like they're worth the effort.

Regardless, you see examples of this everywhere. I'll bet good money that everyone has a goal they secretly would love to accomplish, but they want to make sure the timing is *just right* before they start working on it. They want to make sure they have the time, the money, the motivation, the support — everything in just the right place — before you take any steps forward. You want to give yourself the best chance of success, and I get that.

Maybe it shows up as waiting until Monday to start on a workout regimen — then when Monday is hectic, you decide you'll start next Monday instead. Maybe it's something that's bigger, like waiting to have kids until you can afford them or you're more settled. Maybe it's something that seems a little crazy to you, like writing a book or running an ultra-marathon. Hey, maybe it's just that you make liberal use of the built-in excuse of your husband's long hours and unpredictable schedule, whether they really have a significant impact on your goals or not.

Whatever it is you're putting off for "a better time", it's completely understandable. We all do it sometimes. Ultimately, that procrastination usually boils down to a fear of failure — something we all fear to a certain extent, no matter how self-confident or bulletproof we might appear to be.

Nobody wants to fail. We want to wait to pursue goals until we feel like it's the perfect time. It seems more secure. We want more money, more time, less stress, more security, and more confidence we will succeed.

Waiting until everything is perfect before you start working toward a goal is the absolute best way to make sure you never, ever reach it. There isn't a perfect time for anything. If God wants you to do something, the best possible time to start is right now.

No matter how true that is, it's not fun to start something imperfectly. You want to be the best and not embarrass yourself in front of other people, right? You don't want to be seen as a failure. So let's address that for a minute.

God isn't afraid that you're going to fail. In fact, He knows you're going to fail in your life. Probably a lot. He knows your faults and where you need to grow. He knows what situations you need to be allowed to go through to strengthen the parts of you that are weak[12]. Those weak things only come to light through failure.

Failure is not the fatal thing that we sometimes see it as. When I used to hear people call failure an "opportunity to learn", I thought they were mostly being ironic. I thought of the lessons learned from failure as a consolation prize for messing up, but the reality is, the lessons we learn through failure are the entire point of going through that painful experience. The lessons we learn from failure are the lessons we learn most permanently, and God's whole point in giving us life is allowing us the opportunity to learn and grow.

Look at it this way: were you 100% prepared to become a police wife when you did? Whether your husband was already in law enforcement when you got married or he joined the force a few years in, I'm betting you didn't know everything you were getting into. You didn't have the chance to consider whether the timing was perfect or not. You just did it, because there was no waiting. Your husband was in it, and so were you.

---

[12] *2 Corinthians 12:9-10*

I can tell you for darn sure that I thought I was ready, but I still had a lot of lessons I had to learn from failures. I had to learn all about handling feeling jealous about female partners while being pregnant and insecure. I had to learn to be an easygoing mom from the beginning of motherhood: 8 hours after my C-section, my husband left for mandatory training. I had to learn to be more flexible and not freak out every time plans didn't go like I thought they would.

I would never have learned those lessons without failing at them first. I would never be the woman I am today without the hardships, and God knew that. I definitely felt that He was giving me more than I could handle, but there was a reason for that. He allowed me to go through them so I could learn and get stronger.

Best of all, I know He didn't leave me alone during that time. He guided me through all those struggles and helped me make the decisions I needed to make once I humbled myself enough to ask. Even if I wasn't prepared for the task He gave me, He led me through it and guided me to be who I needed to be.

Whether the things God is calling you to feel like a small step out in faith or a giant leap off a cliff, hold tight to the promise that no matter how hopeless and unsure things seem, God will always uphold you. Don't wait until conditions are perfect. Just get started, even if you're scared. Take the first step and prayerfully put one foot in front of the other until you get to where you want to be – and most importantly, where God wants you to be.

Trust Him through all your fumbles and missteps. Know that He knows what you need to learn, and is pretty great at teaching you those lessons in ways you'll understand most. When things get hard, don't forget that He's always there for you, will never let you down, and has promised that He only intends good things for you.

Most of all, don't spend your life waiting for life to be perfect before you get started. If you do that, I guarantee that a year from now, you'll be glad you got started when you did, so get moving!

# PRAYER IDEAS

- Thank God for the comfort that comes from His promise that He only intends good things for you.
- Thank God for every opportunity He's given you to turn your weaknesses into strength.
- Ask to know if there's something He has in mind for you to do — starting right now.
- If there's a goal you have in mind that you feel you'd like to pursue, ask whether it's in line with His will.  If so, ask for help pursuing it.
- Pray for the courage to get started even when you're scared.
- Pray for His comfort as you move forward in faith.

# PURPOSEFUL
# BE PREPARED

*When it snows, she has no fear for her household;*
*for all of them are clothed in scarlet.*
*Proverbs 31:21*

As a police wife, you see your husband prepare for worst case scenarios all the time. He has to think about what could go wrong so that if it does, he's ahead of it. He has a plan in place that he can just implement automatically if a dangerous situation arises. He doesn't want to be scrambling and caught off guard if it were to happen, even if the possibility is relatively remote.

It's why you get "the look" from him when you sit in the wrong spot at the restaurant, because he's already determined that seat to have the best tactical advantage. He's assessed the situation and developed a rough plan for what he would do in case of an emergency, and he's not about to let you get in the way of implementing that plan. It's an act of love, even if it gets annoying sometimes.

It's a little intense sometimes, but it has its advantages for sure. The annoyance it presents at times is worth the knowledge that your husband knows what he's going to do if something terrible happens. His preparation gives you peace of mind – and, over time, prepares you to think the same way. Maybe not as thoroughly, but I'd say definitely more than the average woman.

Seriously, my husband has me so well-trained that people can't really sneak up on me anymore. I'm too used to using any available reflective surface to see what's going on around me. It's kind of funny to see how far I've come over the years of watching him do the same thing. But back to the point.

The Proverbs 31 wife actually has a lot in common with your husband, believe it or not. She prepares for disasters (even snow, as referenced in the above scripture) in advance. She is painted as being such a wise, faithful woman, though, that I don't for a second believe she's only prepared for the inevitability of winter. I have a feeling she was prepared for other emergencies, too.

That doesn't mean she anxiously wrings her hands thinking about everything that could go wrong. Not at all! Picture your husband when he's assessing tactical advantage at a restaurant. He thinks about what could happen not out of fear that something will happen, just out of wanting to be prepared if it does. Neither your husband nor the Proverbs 31 wife want to be caught blindsided in the case of emergency.

Both types of preparation offer comfort. Both are important. And while your husband is in a good position to prepare in advance for the safety of your family, you happen to be in a great position to prepare like the Proverbs 31 wife. You can make sure your home and family are prepared for every kind of emergency.

Before I go any further, I want to address a myth I've heard in the past about preparing for emergencies. I've heard it said that preparing for emergencies spells a lack of faith, because you're not putting your faith in God to take care of you. I don't see it that way at all.

Prayerfully preparing for your family's temporal needs means you can partner with Him to care for those you love most. It's not about looking outside of His goodness for protection. It's about helping Him to help you if the worst were to happen[13]. Prepare out of faith, not out of fear.

The key is to prepare prayerfully. It's going to look so different for every family, and it's easy to fall down the "doomsday prepper" rabbit hole if you're not careful. Maybe extreme preparation feels right for your family, but chances are you don't need to go that far. I'm pretty confident the Proverbs 31 wife isn't intense about things because she doesn't have the time (seriously – no electric washer and dryer!), and you don't have to, either.

There are a few things you might want to think about, though:

### Assembling an emergency kit/go bag.

FEMA is, of course, a great resource to find out what you should keep on hand for emergencies, like what kind of food and how much water, that kind of thing. Seeing hurricanes and wildfires all over the country might inspire you to do what you can to prepare, and it's not a bad idea at all.

You can see the what they recommend at fema.org.

### Having an emergency exit plan for household emergencies.

Having a plan for a house fire or intruder isn't a bad idea, either. Your husband might already have his own plan for if that happens, but if you don't know what it is, it's not all that useful. Getting on the same page before any emergency actually becomes a reality is totally worth it.

---

[13] *Ezekiel 38:7*

## Life insurance.

It's not fun to think about, but life insurance provides peace of mind for if the worst were to happen to you or your husband. Talking about the hard stuff before you actually need it is way better than scrambling when you do, especially because you would be dealing with heartache and trauma on top of all the logistics of life.

Make sure you have enough life insurance taken out on *both* of you, by the way. When we first got life insurance on one another, the amount for mine was lower because I didn't work. Over time, I've realized it needs to be equal to or more than his because of all the little services I do around the house that he'd suddenly need to cover – like daycare, cleaning, food costs, etc. All those expenses would suddenly increase, and I wouldn't want to leave him in a bind.

## An emergency fund.

The standard amount I've heard is $1000, but again, this is a completely personal matter. Having any amount of money set aside will help in case either of you lose your job or get injured, and the amount you can afford or need to set aside is between you, your husband, and God.

The main point I want to make here is that when you know you have a plan for the things that could happen, you can rest easy knowing those things won't kill you. It means you don't have to worry about uncertainty when it comes to natural disasters, or even financial disasters. It can reduce your anxiety and help you focus on the things that matter most if disaster strikes.

Whatever it is, prayerfully preparing for hard times when things are good means you can live feeling more secure. You can know that if the worst happens, you can focus on your family and God and not worry as much about your temporal needs. It's an amazing time investment, one the Proverbs 31 wife makes sure she doesn't neglect.

That being said, preparing for temporal needs in the face of a disaster is only part of what you can prepare for. You can also use times of peace in your relationships to prepare for storms — especially when it comes to your marriage.

I love the comparison of your marriage to a bank account. When times are good, you can make "love deposits" that can help hold you over when times get trying. While it's hard to predict everything you'll need to prepare for in your marriage, those deposits are easy enough to make. They consist of the small, nice, everyday things that show your husband you love and respect him. You can choose to do nice things that are important to him so that it can withstand whatever storms come your way, whether they come in the form of a complication of his job like being switched to night shift, financial strain, or the general stresses of life.

Honestly, they don't take much. A simple "please" or "thank you" can go a long way, for instance. I love when my husband thanks me for doing something mundane, like folding the laundry, because it makes me feel recognized and appreciated. He loves when I put down my work for a while and snuggle with him while we watch something (even if it's something I don't necessarily "get", like football.)

The deposits you make in your marriage will look different depending on what you and your husband value most, but regardless, they can be simple enough. Usually, they don't take a lot of time — they just take intention.

Some other examples:

- Packing his lunch and leaving a nice note in it.
- Setting electronics aside to have a true heart-to-heart conversation.
- Commenting on how good he looks in his uniform.
- Telling him how proud you are of him.
- Giving him a shoulder massage after a stressful shift.

This is definitely not an exhaustive list. You know your husband best, so follow his cues when it comes to what he wants most from you. You can consult God on this issue, too, since He is deeply interested in the success of your marriage. Plus, He knows your husband better than you do. Who better to ask?

When you're feeling hurt, try to center your mind on the deposits he's made in the past. Think about the nice things he has done for you before, and remember how much he loves you. Knowing he has made investments in your relationship in the past can help the hurts of today feel a lot less important.

When it comes to your other relationships, you can follow the same principle. It's amazing how far a quick, "hey, how are you?" text message goes to feeding a friendship. The occasional unexpected "yes" to your kids' requests can help them see you as more of an advocate and less of a barrier to the stuff they want (which I have no doubt my son sometimes sees me as!)

You can also prepare yourself emotionally for the storms of life. You can take the time you need to rest, recuperate, and reconnect with yourself, your family, and your God. Don't let yourself get so busy that you forget to feed your soul. When times are good, you can learn more about God so that you're more prepared for when the bad stuff comes. You can prepare to come closer to Him, not fall away when things get hard.

If you hope for the best but prepare for the worst, you will be better able to deal with issues as they arise. Sure, there will always be things that come up that you completely didn't expect, but the more you do in advance, the more you can offset the impact of those troubles on your life.

Being prepared for all situations allows you to worry less and focus on God more, because you'll know everything else is taken care of. Best of all, by prayerfully preparing for physical or emotional disasters in your life, you know without a doubt you will be prepared if something happens. He'll be able to bless you and make up the difference if you're short on anything, as long as you've been obedient to Him.

Thinking about the future and how you can make things as secure as possible is undoubtedly a hallmark of the Proverbs 31 wife.

# PRAYER IDEAS

- Thank God for the promise that He will always take care of you.
- Thank God for the opportunity to partner with Him in preparing your family for emergencies.
- Ask for the wisdom to know what to prepare your family for and how.
- Ask for peace as you consider those possibilities so that you can do so out of faith, not fear.
- Ask Him to help feed the important relationships in your life to sustain you for when things get hard.

# HUMBLE

*Charm is deceptive and beauty is fleeting;*
*but a woman who fears the Lord is to be praised.*
*Proverbs 31:30*

Humility has been an interesting subject for me ever since I first found Christ. That wasn't until my early twenties, so frankly, I had a lot to learn. When I heard the virtues of humility being praised in church and in the scriptures, I had a lot of questions about what exactly that meant. I had no idea.

When I pondered it, I thought about my self-esteem issues in my childhood and teen years. Was that humility? That didn't feel quite right, especially when I realized that insecurity made me prone to gossiping about other people to make myself feel a little better. Obviously, being a jerk to other people isn't the defining trait of humility.

There was another part of me that wondered if humility was a sign of being inherently weak. Even though it was praised as a Godly trait, I didn't necessarily want to think of myself as being weak. One thing I've always liked about myself is my willingness to speak up on others' behalf when they're being mistreated. I wasn't sure if my boldness was something that offended God, but I didn't like to think of it that way. That thought just didn't quite resonate with me.

I realized over time that the reason I was having such issues with determining what humility means is because it's such a vast, multifaceted subject. It's not just about one aspect of someone's personality: it presents itself in different ways. It has as many variations to it as its opposite, pride, does.

I learned over time that humility is mainly about understanding your place in the grand scheme of things, and especially in relation to God. It's about being realistic about what your strengths and weaknesses are without excessive pride or self-flagellation about either of them. It's about acknowledging that God gave you both your strength and weaknesses, and He gave them to you for a reason.

True humility isn't rooted in weakness, but in finding your strength in God. It's about living your life with intense gratitude for him and reverence for what He has to say to you. It's not about being silent or passive, but speaking up for and fighting the battles that He asks you to fight because you see yourself as His servant first and foremost.

It means you recognize the gifts God has given you, express gratitude for them, and use them to help others in need. You understand that He didn't give you those abilities just to make you look awesome to the world, but so that you could be uniquely useful to Him as a servant. You don't take pride in your own abilities, but give all glory to God for giving them to you.

Being humble means that no matter what you have to forsake – whether that's your reputation, your desires, or anything you think you want the most – you're willing to let those things go in order to obey God in all circumstances. You're willing to let Him use you for the things He needs to accomplish in this world, because you have the utmost trust that He always intends good for you.

True humility is about being teachable. It's what allows you to progress as His disciple, because it's what allows you to listen to His spirit and act accordingly. If you're too wrapped up in your own pride, it's not possible to listen to and act on the plans He has in store for you. You're too busy hearing yourself think to hear what He has to say.

Christ was the perfect example of humility[14]. He willingly sacrificed everything for the glory of God. He spent His life serving those around Him. He suffered the pain of the cross to allow God's plan of redemption to come to pass, and never even spoke a harsh word about being put in that situation. He asked that if it were possible to have the bitter cup pass that it would be, but said if not, He would submit to His Father's will.

My initial concern that humility was a sign of weakness was so completely off-base it's laughable. Choosing to be humble is the greatest strength we can have in this world, because it more fully allows God to use us for the things that the world needs[15]. Not only that, it allows us the opportunity to become the people He wants us to be, because we've decided that He knows best and have committed to following in His ways.

There's a reason the verse at the beginning of this chapter says that while beauty and charm are fleeting, a woman who fears the Lord is to be praised. The humble, God-fearing woman has access to the greatest power in the universe. She can be an indomitable force for good, and the man who's by her side will undoubtedly be blessed by her example[16].

Becoming truly, perfectly humble isn't a natural process. As human beings, we're not naturally humble. Even if you don't think of yourself as a prideful person (not like that pain in the butt who lives

---

[14] *Philippians 2:5-8*
[15] *James 3:10*
[16] *Proverbs 31:28*

down the street and constantly brags about how awesome she is, right?), there's a good chance you possess more pride than you realize.

Being prideful can be thinking too much about yourself, even if it's in the form of self-flagellating thoughts. If you're so distracted by your own positive or negative characteristics that you can't reach out to help others, you're allowing pride to cloud your view. True humility means thinking less of yourself and more about what the people around you need.

At the same time, pridefulness can also mean being too wrapped up with what others think of you rather than focusing on what God thinks of you. If you are being meek and bowing down to the people around you and not God, that's not being humble. God's opinion matters more than anyone else's, and it's important that you never forget that.

A lack of humility can also be thinking you know what's best and ignoring good advice to the contrary, simply because you want to be able to say, "I did it all by myself." It's failing to acknowledge that any good thing that comes in your life is a gift from God, not something that came from you being just that awesome.

Judging other people without taking into account how similar you might be to them is another example of pride. When you assume their actions and motivations are completely different from yours and fail to take into account the fact that they are human and imperfect, too, you're failing to recognize your own imperfections. Not only that, but you're also missing a great opportunity to help when you're focused on judging instead.

It's important to recognize these shades of humility to make sure you avoid the traps of being overly prideful and take advantage of all the blessings God has to offer you. This chapter is all about developing a greater attitude of humility in your life.

# SECTIONS

Don't Compare Yourself to Others
Grateful in Every Circumstance
Seek to Understand, Not Control
Progress, Not Perfection

# HUMBLE
## DON'T COMPARE YOURSELF TO OTHERS

*Pay careful attention to your own work, for then you will get the satisfaction of a job well done, and you won't need to compare yourself to anyone else.  For we are each responsible for our own conduct.*
*Galatians 6:4-5 (NLT)*

Even though it's awesome that we can connect so quickly and easily with each other in this day and age, the downside to that is that when we do so through Facebook or Instagram, we tend to only see the awesome parts of other people's lives – not their full story.  That means when we naturally compare those things to our own lives, they just don't match up.

Honestly, it's just the nature of the social media beast.  It's not just those who are facetious about their lives who make us jealous.  It's simply the fact that you tend to share the best things online because that's what you want to remember.  Those are the things you want people to know about you most, and that's not inherently an issue.

The thing is, because we're seeing this skewed views of other people's lives, it's more common than ever to covet what other people have. Whether that's someone else's money situation, someone else's kids, someone else's job, someone else's husband's propensity toward bringing them flowers all the time, whatever. It's easy to look at what other people have and wonder why you don't get to have it, too.

True story: I've been jealous about other people getting flowers, too. I've thought to myself, "Why doesn't my husband bring me flowers all the time like theirs does?" Do you want to know what's ridiculous about that? I don't even like receiving flowers. Seriously, my husband knows that if he gives me some, I smile and say thank you, but I secretly feel annoyed knowing I'll just have to throw them out in a week. It's less of a gift to me and more of an extra chore on my to-do list.

I can admit that it's completely irrational, but at the same time, it's understandable to want to get not only the romantic gesture, but also the attention that comes from sharing the good stuff on social media. When I'm in a lousy mood, seeing the good news of other people can make my bad stuff feel even worse. I want something good to share, darn it!

When I have good stuff to share but see someone else with better status updates, it can put a damper on my excitement. It can make me feel envious and bitter because I didn't get what they got. It happens even if I'm super excited about my news.

It's something I'm working on, but I've had to unfollow pretty much everyone on social media. I still have it because I use it for work, but when I don't see anyone's status updates, it forces me to actually connect with people. Those personal connections feel more loving and less comparison-filled, and that's just what I have to do for my own sanity.

Theodore Roosevelt puts it wonderfully succinctly when he says, "Comparison is the thief of joy." It's 100% true. When you compare yourself to others, it sucks all the joy out of all the good things you have by casting it in the light of what other people have. It makes you less grateful for all the blessings in your life, and instead focuses your attention on what you feel you might be lacking.

As a police wife, your life probably looks a lot different from the way you might have pictured it as a little girl. Most little girls never dreamed their knight in shining armor would be absent at family events, super stressed out all the time, and barely even be home for dinner at night. When you see your non-police wife friends who don't have to deal with those things, it's understandable to get a little jealous. There are a lot of things about your life that make your bare minimum harder than theirs, no matter what extra stuff each of you has to deal with.

Normal is relative. The key to rocking this life is accepting your life as *your* normal and loving it for what it is (and treating yourself to a nice hot bubble bath and chocolate when it's just not possible.) If you look at the blessings in your life compared to other people's, your focus is going to be less on making the most of what you have, and more on griping about what you don't.

God gave you this life for a reason. He gave you the trials you face specifically for you. None of the things that have happened to you were by accident, and nothing that will ever happen will be by accident, either. He is mindful of you. He knows what you need, both right now and in the long run, and He gives you both gifts and challenges based on those things.

As you develop the humility necessary to accept your own life as it is and make it the best you can, you'll find all the energy you used focusing on what other people are doing is way more efficiently used on your own problems. Any time spent moaning about the unfairness of life won't get you where you want to be, whether it's about your marriage, your children, your job, anything. If you want to get anywhere, you have to stop focusing on what other people are doing and put that energy where it belongs.

Sometimes God will help you change those things quickly. Sometimes He'll allow you to languish in a situation because you haven't learned all the lessons you need to from it. Either way, when your energy is focused where it matters, you will end up having a happier life.

The other significant issue with comparing yourself to others is that you don't actually understand what you're comparing yourself to, since you're seeing a small sliver of other people's situations. A few months ago, I was talking with other moms and we had a really eye-opening conversation about our struggles. We talked candidly about our failures, our struggles, all the times we felt like we were failing, and all the things we wish we were better at. It was an incredible experience.

You see, lots of these women are ones I've felt jealous of when seeing their social media posts. I thought they were just perfect, with perfect lives, but when I understood they fail in many of the same ways I do, it was sobering. I'd always heard to take what you read on social media with a grain of salt, that it's just a highlight reel, but that discussion was extremely powerful in how I view social media posts now.

Always, always, always remember that when you see a status on Facebook, you're only seeing a part of the picture, not someone's complete story. You probably have more struggles in common than you realize, which means you can help each other out rather than stew in jealousy about what the other has.

Comparing yourself to others really does take away your joy. I know it's a hard habit to break (after all, I wrote this just as much for myself as anybody else), but today is the day to work on recognizing it and working on replacing your feelings of envy with feelings of gratitude.

You might do that through praying more intentionally about your blessings. Maybe you have a planner you use regularly that you could write your daily blessings in. Maybe you really want to make gratitude a priority in your life and you start a full-on gratitude journal. How you work on changing this attitude is up to you, but doing something to focus more on gratitude will make your life a thousand times better, without you even having to change anything.

Recognize that God loves you and will always provide you with what you need. Recognize that your life is different from everyone else's, and that fair isn't about everyone getting the same thing, but everyone getting what they need.

Truly, God will never steer you wrong.

# PRAYER IDEAS

- Thank God for having the perfect plan for you and your life, even when things don't make much sense to you.
- Thank God for loving you for you, not as you compare to anybody else, and ask for help doing the same.
- Ask for the eyes to see your blessings clearly, not through a lens of comparison to the blessings of others.
- Ask for help learning to celebrate the successes of others, rather than feeling jealous of them.
- Ask for help reducing your inclination to compare yourself to others in general.

# HUMBLE
## GRATEFUL IN EVERY CIRCUMSTANCE

*I will extol the Lord at all times; His praise will always be on my lips.*
*Psalm 34:1*

The story of Job is pretty incredible. He's this perfect man, with everything he could ever want, who perfectly worships God. Satan suggests to God that if He were to take all those things away, Job wouldn't be quite so obedient. He suspects the only reason Job is so good is because he doesn't want for anything. God then allows Satan to test Job, and as a result, Job loses everything. He loses his fortune, his property, his children, his friends, his relationship with his wife – absolutely everything.

In response, he actually praises God[17]. He doesn't curse him or blame Him for all the bad things that have happened to him. He accepts that God is in control and that He knows best. He acknowledges that God is always good, even when his life is crashing down all around him.

I'd like you to put yourself in Job's shoes for a second. How do you think you might respond to these trials? Do you think you'd fall to

---

[17] *Job 1:20-21*

your knees in praise to your God, or do you think you'd raise your fist and ask why He'd be so mean to you?

Be honest: nobody's judging you here.

Besides, I'd be the last person who could judge you for leaning toward the latter. While I'd love to say I could be like Job and praise God even under such extreme hardship, I don't really know that I could. Based on prior hard times in my life, I have my suspicions I would lean that way, too. I will say that after the trials we've experienced in the past few years, I'm more able to come close to Him when life is hard than I ever could before.

However, don't think that spiritual growth came easily. It came through soul-crushing disappointment. It came through job losses, unexpected expenses, being dirt poor, being scammed, having things stolen from us, and even, most recently, a miscarriage. I can tell you that through all those experiences, I had a lot of questions for God. At times, I had a lot of anger. My prayers have been filled with some choice words at times, so I'm super grateful for His unending capacity for forgiveness.

As much as these experiences hurt, every single one of them has grown my faith by leaps and bounds. I can tell you with a certainty I'm incredibly different from the woman I was three years ago. I'm more patient, more resilient, more humble, and I have a better understanding of the complexity and goodness of God.

God put me through the ringer in order to help me grow and be better. The pain was worth it. It was for my good, even when I didn't understand. I'm not sure if I can say I glory in tribulations[18], but if you asked me if I would undo those experiences if I could, I'd give you a firm no. I would never trade those experiences for anything because I

---

[18] *Romans 5:3*

would never want to undo the changes God has worked in me. I wouldn't take any of it back.

Through those disappointments, I've learned that there are two important things you need to remember in order to remain grateful to God, no matter what circumstance you're facing.

First of all, you need to remember that God is always looking out for you. He's interested in the minutiae of your life. He cares about how you're doing, whether it's good or bad. When you're happy, he's happy, too. When you cry, he's there to catch your tears. When you're in a valley of darkness in life and you feel like you're all alone, you've got to remember that it's only a feeling. God has never, and will never, leave your side, unless you ask Him to (and even then, he stays right on the sidelines, waiting to be invited back.)

Seriously, He's not a detached or lazy God. He's not kicked back, relaxed while watching the awful things that happen to you. He doesn't sigh and think, "Well, that's a bummer. Best of luck." That's not how it is at all!

Remember that He knows literally everything about you. He knows the things that nobody else knows – or will ever know. He knows your thoughts, your secrets, your desires, your prayers, the hairs on your head, everything. He wouldn't let things happen to you without having His say in the situation.

If you can find nothing to be grateful for in a terrible situation, focus on that. Know that He sees you in every situation and is always, always there for you. He'll never leave you or forsake you.[19] Don't let yourself think otherwise, because that's Satan trying to dissuade you from the course God has set for you.

---

[19] *Deuteronomy 31:6*

You can also take comfort in the fact that God is the God of victories. If you look closely, no matter how dark your world appears at first, you'll see He's provided for silver linings to be all around you. Even if those victories are only silver linings for a while and not huge advances forward, you can take comfort in knowing that He will always get you through what you're going through.

Second of all, you need to remember that God doesn't actually owe you anything. Seriously. He owes you nothing, yet He's willing to give you everything. He's willing to wipe your slate clean and offer complete forgiveness for every bad thing you've ever done, no matter how horrendous. Once you've fully repented, He even promises to forget it ever happened.[20] He's willing to comfort you in every circumstance, even if it's something you brought upon yourself. He's willing to love you, completely, even when you're an unloveable mess. He wants you, as small and imperfect as you are.

Isn't that amazing? That's a serious testament to how much He actually loves you. Because if you're anything like me, you're thinking, "He loves me despite *that*?" Whatever that "that" is, I can assure you: yes, He does.

If you can start looking at the blessings you receive from Him not as things you've earned by being so faithful and instead recognize them as completely extra, the times when things aren't so good are put in some serious perspective. It can help you find peace in both the hills and valleys of life.

If you're having trouble seeing the silver linings, or even the outright blessings in your life, it can help to get outside of your own situation for a while. You could confide your struggles to a friend and ask for their perspective. You could also forget your issues altogether and spend some time serving someone – whether they're just a

---

[20] *Hebrews 8:12*

neighbor who could use a little extra help or someone in a homeless/women's shelter who has way more significant issues than you. Either way, the experience will shed new light on your own problems.

In every situation, remember Him. When you're on top of the world, remember who brought you there and allowed it to happen, and be grateful to Him for everything He's given you. When you're brought low and things aren't so great, remember all the times He's gotten you through and remember that nothing that happens is for naught.

Remember the truth of who God truly is, at all times, and in all circumstances, and always raise your hands in praise for His goodness. Trust that God is always working things for your good and be determined to follow what He asks of you, knowing that He will hold you up and make everything work for your good.

# PRAYER IDEAS

- Thank God for all the good things He's given you in your life, and for working all the bad things for your long-term benefit.
- Thank God for loving you, despite every fault you have.
- Thank God for the opportunities to be tried and tested that bring you closer to Him.
- Ask for help seeing the silver linings in tough situations.
- If you're in the midst of a crisis, ask Him to reveal to you what you need to learn from the situation.
- Ask for help coming closer to Him when you feel like pulling away – and whenever you feel like pulling away, pray *something* instead.  The smallest effort will make a big difference.
- Pray with complete honesty about your feelings – whether they're sadness, anger, confusion, or anything.  Trust that He loves you and is big enough to handle everything you've got for Him.

# HUMBLE
## SEEK TO UNDERSTAND, NOT CONTROL

*Jesus answered him, "What I am doing you do not understand
now, but afterward you will understand."*
*John 13:7*

I don't necessarily like to think of myself as a controlling person, but I really, really like it when things go exactly as I'd planned. For instance, I love drawing out elaborate plans every New Year's Eve about all the things I want to do, and have these fantastic dreams of how perfect this year is going to be.

Take 2018 for instance. I got a huge black poster board, a chalk pen to make it look pretty, and wrote out a gigantic laundry list of goals I wanted to accomplish this year. I knew some of them were stretch goals, but I actually felt pretty confident about meeting at least most of them. Silly me.

Someday as I'm doing this, I'll actually remember that phrase about how if you want to make God laugh, you just have to tell him your plans. I'm currently writing this in September of 2018, and my poster board of aspirations is embarrassingly incomplete. I have less than 4 months to meet those goals, and the chances aren't looking all that great. The goal I'm closest to meeting is reading 30 books this year, and my need for a daily nap at this stage of pregnancy comes before my need to read.

Seriously, I think I'll get to 2019 without hitting a single goal this year besides, "get my taxes done before February."

Without a doubt, every time I make elaborate plans with the intention of executing them perfectly, something or other gets in the way and I don't get things exactly as I wanted. It's incredibly frustrating at times, but I've realized that one of the big lessons God is teaching me is how to be able to go with the flow more easily.

He's taught that to me for many years — probably starting with how long it took my husband to get hired with a police department. I think it was either 4 or 5 years. When he finally got hired, it was kind of last minute. I couldn't believe the whirlwind of training and excitement. Then, of course, police wife life does a really good job of teaching you to be okay with life not going according to plan, since even your mundane day-to-day plans usually don't.

I don't believe for one instant that being a police wife and the drastic life changes that came from that point on were by accident. What I know in my heart, and what gets me through every difficulty and disappointment, is that we love and live for a God who has everything all planned out. He may not have it planned out as linearly as we think it should be, but even when the plans appear to be messy and nonsensical, every intricacy of His plan is perfectly thought out, because He knows and sees everything.

Maybe you've struggled with the same thing. You might have had the desire to control everything from your perspective, especially when it comes to your husband's line of work. Maybe you didn't even want him to become a police officer at all at first, because you know so much would be outside your control. Yet, when it came down to it, for whatever reason, you knew it was the right move for him. Regardless of your reservations, he went ahead.

Maybe the process leaves you wondering at times whether it's what he (and you) were really meant for. Couldn't you have a simpler life, like someone married to, say, a banker? Or hey, even one with a little more money, like someone married to an engineer. Why did police wife life, of all things, have to be in your life's plan?

When you look at the broad scope of other peoples' lives, the fingerprints of God are sometimes extremely obvious. It's easy to see those long-term plans when you're not actually in the situation. Unfortunately, that isn't always true when it comes to our own lives. We're too close and can't always see what He's trying to do for us, even if we can see how He's working in other people's lives.

In the long run, even though it can be frustrating, that's completely normal and okay. As long as you focus on trusting Him, things will eventually make sense. Trust that even if you can't understand what He's doing right now, He'll eventually make everything perfectly clear to you[21]. If you stay faithful, everything will work out as it should, and you'll end up being so grateful He had such an awesome plan.

Remember that humility means being teachable[22]. That means choosing to accept that while His ways aren't our ways, His ways are perfect. It means accepting that your plans may not be His plans, but that even when your plans you go desperately awry, He has better ones in store. He has the plans for you that will be for your eternal well-being, that will make you the happiest – in the long run, at least. They might not feel like they make you happy right now, and that's normal, too.

I relate this a lot to being a parent to my child. He doesn't always understand the rules I make or the reasons behind them. Even if I

---

[21] *John 13:7*
[22] *Psalm 25:9*

explained them until I was blue in the face, he wouldn't have the maturity to understand the long-term benefits I know about.

I can tell you that as soon as I'm done writing this, he will inevitably start his daily hardcore questioning of the wisdom behind naptimes. He doesn't understand that the small time investment of not playing will result in him being happier afterward. He doesn't really understand that Mommy will be less cranky afterward, too. He doesn't always understand what his body needs. He doesn't know everything I know. Likewise, we don't know and see all the things God does, which is why we just need to trust Him.

The trick is to pray about the things you're struggling to understand, and (unlike my toddler) listen to what God has to say about the situation. He'll happily give you an answer a lot of the time. There are times He may not be ready to tell you yet, because you wouldn't understand. If that's the case, He might grant you a sense of peace about things instead, so that you can know things will work out, even if you're not sure how.

When either of these two things happen, you can move on to praying about what you need to do next. He will bless your willingness to act in faith, whether you understand why things are happening the way they are or not. God can't lie to you or misdirect you, or He would cease to be God[23]. Since He isn't ever going to cease to be God, you can trust in whatever direction He provides you.

When you seek to understand God's will rather than control it, you'll find yourself coming closer to Him every day. You'll find greater peace in the tumultuous times in your life. You'll have a greater ability to make it through those times with your sanity and faith intact. You'll find more joy, even when life is at its darkest. Joy can always be found if you know where to look.

---

[23] *Hebrews 6:17-18*

Be humble enough to accept that He does know what's best for you. Have the faith to know He loves you enough to make sure the best things are what happens for you, even if you have to get a little hurt in the process. Trust that He will not let anything happen to you that isn't for your good.

Let your circumstances teach you about faith, courage, love, charity, selflessness, forgiveness, and all the things He wants you to learn more about in this life. He will always lead you the right way if you choose to be humble enough to seek to understand His ways and not conform them to what you think is right.

# PRAYER IDEAS

- Thank God for having a plan for your life – and affirm that you trust that He does.
- Thank God for not always bending to what you want, but for sticking to what you need because He knows best.
- Admit to God you always need Him to guide you to make the best decisions.
- Ask for help in letting your plans go and embracing His, even when they don't make sense.
- Ask for your heart to be softened toward His will for your life.
- Ask for understanding or peace when the situations in your life don't make sense to you.

# HUMBLE
# PROGRESS, NOT PERFECTION

*But grow in the grace and knowledge of our Lord and Savior Jesus*
*Christ. To him be glory both now and forever! Amen.*
*2 Peter 3:18*

I've always been a perfectionist to a fault. You wouldn't know
necessarily know it by looking at me, because I don't have the typical
type A personality. My house is usually a mess, especially when it
comes to my workspaces. I like to have everything strewn in front of
me.

As a teenager, you might have thought I just didn't care. I made
jokes about bad grades on tests I'd worked hard on to cover up the
fact that it made me so ashamed. I couldn't understand why my hard
work didn't pay off like it seemed to for other people. Despite my
strengths in certain subjects, my failure in others stood out to me way
more. I felt like I was inherently defective.

As an adult, I've still spent most of my time setting impossible
standards for myself to live up to. I want to do everything, be
everything to everyone, and never miss a beat. I want to be that
person who never gets tired or needs a break.

Naturally, I don't meet those standards, and it wasn't until I found
Christ that I started to question how hard I was on myself. It's been a

few years and I still have a long way to go, but I had an experience recently that made me realize how far I've actually come.

To make a long story short, I misjudged what the person in front of me was going to do at a green light and rear-ended them. It was super minor, as we couldn't have been going more than ten miles per hour, but it was still enough of an impact that they, in turn, rear-ended the person in front of them.

As soon as I hit, I was mortified. My old feelings of inadequacy rose up in my mind, especially because my son started bawling immediately. I felt like a failure as a mom, a person, a driver... needless to say, I spiraled fast, because that's just my default. I'd love to say I've grown out of it, but I know it's something that takes time. And, of course, the pregnancy hormones didn't necessarily help.

I called my husband after I'd pulled off into a nearby parking lot and cried my eyes out. He told me he was on his way, and asked me to take some deep breaths. He told me everything was okay, that even if all three cars had been totaled in the accident, he wouldn't be mad. He was just glad none of us were hurt.

My head knew it wasn't a big deal in the long run. My head knew everyone makes mistakes, that I'm not the only one to ever make a mistake while driving, and that it doesn't say anything about me as a person. I could think that logically through. Unfortunately, my heart stuck by the idea that I was the worst person ever.

When the officer responded, it was embarrassing, but seriously – the accident was so minor. It wasn't *that* big of a deal. I was found 100% at fault, which stung, but I tried to gracefully accept it. The officer gave me a citation for following too closely, and I cried. I wasn't mad or upset at him – I just felt guilty because I wished that money could have gone elsewhere.

As we left the scene, I shook the officer's hand and said thank you. I appreciated his helpfulness after the accident and I knew how much paperwork he'd have to deal with as a result of my actions. I didn't blame him for the ticket at all, because, of course, it was my own stupid mistake that got me into the mess.

As I did, he smiled at me and said, "It happens."

When my husband drove me home, I commented that the officer giving me a citation just gave me more grace than I've ever shown myself. Ever. The thought kind of made me laugh — because in all honesty, that officer should have been the one judging me the most harshly.

Even though it wasn't easy, I tried to take that opportunity to learn to show myself grace. Even though I still felt guilty (and sore, because even in a minor accident, my body wasn't happy about it), I tried to focus instead on thinking, "It's okay. Everyone makes mistakes. No matter what comes of it, it's going to be okay."

While that night was difficult, I woke up the next morning feeling refreshed (albeit even sorer, darn it). I knew I'd turned a page in terms of my personal development, and giving myself that grace changed everything. When my son spilled his drink at lunch time, I had a moment of frustration, then said, "It's okay, sweetie. Everyone makes mistakes. Let's clean it up."

Seriously, God is an excellent teacher who knows just how to make His point in a way we understand best. It's kind of mind-blowing to think of everything I was able to take away from that moment of misjudgment, because He even managed to work *that* for my good.

Trust me when I say I understand how paralyzing it can be to want to be perfect all the time. When you want to do everything perfectly lest you berate yourself for not measuring up, it's easier not to do anything at all. There's nothing wrong with taking pride in your work, but when that perfectionism becomes toxic, it's like being in a prison. It limits your options immensely, for no other reason than you're worried someone might judge you for being imperfect.

Being overly concerned with perfection means you're probably missing out on the lessons you could be learning in the process. If you allow yourself to find joy in your mistakes (even if you have to cry a little about it first), life becomes a whole lot more fun. Because life just isn't that much fun when someone's being mean to you all the time.

All God truly cares about is your forward progress. He knows your starting point, and when you're at the end, He'll see that, too. In the middle, when you're in the midst of trial and error, He cares about the lessons you're learning. He cares about the times you fail inasmuch as they teach you what you need to learn. He cares about the times you succeed, because He wants to be there to celebrate with you.

Remember that God never intended for us to be perfect. He created us knowing we would fall short. He knew we would make mistakes – oh my gosh, *so many* mistakes. That's why we needed Christ to die for us in the first place. He knew every one of us would need it, no matter how "good" we are.

I realize that you carry a lot of weight in your life because your husband is gone a lot. It's easy to feel like you need to be perfect in everything you do at home to make up for the fact that he's not there. Even with that being the case, know that you're still worth everything to God. Your efforts are still enough for Him.

When you doubt your worth during times of failure, remember that He knows every mistake you've made. He knows every mistake you've even thought about making. He knows every single one of your imperfections, probably even better than you do, and He still loves you completely.

When you make mistakes, whether they're major or minor, remember you can always come to Him in repentance. You can admit when you've chosen the wrong thing, ask for forgiveness, and ask for guidance on how to make things right[24]. Some of the most tender moments I've had with God have been ones during which I've been turning to him with an admission of guilt. Even if all you've done wrong is you feel guilty over an impulse purchase when you should have used the money elsewhere (been there!), the love and peace you'll feel from Him when you humbly repent is overwhelming.

Ultimately, He doesn't care that much about the mistake you've made. He cares much more about how we react to the mistake. It's whether we try to hide it[25] – a la Cain and Abel – or whether we come right to Him and admit we fell short, then ask Him to help us. He wants your heart more than anything else.

Don't let your fear of not being good enough hold you back from doing what you can. Trust that God has equipped you with all the tools you need right now, and that through His plan for you, you'll develop everything else you need when the time comes. Know that only His opinion of you truly matters, no matter how noisy your critics become. They don't know you, your story, or how everything will work out in the end: He does. Press forward in faith and know that He'll undoubtedly take care of the rest.

---

[24] *2 Chronicles 7:14*
[25] *Proverbs 28:13*

# PRAYER IDEAS

- Thank God for being understanding about your shortcomings and always being willing to show you grace.
- Thank God for the opportunity to repent and become better.
- Ask for help showing yourself grace for your mistakes and focusing on learning from them.
- If there's a mistake you've made that you need to make right, ask for His guidance on how best to do so.

# FULL OF FAITH

*She is clothed with strength and dignity,*
*and she laughs without fear of the future.*
*Proverbs 31:25 (NLT)*

Faith in God is a tricky subject for police wives. Even though it's essential to keeping your sanity while your husband is off saving the world, it's also hard to maintain because of all the evil he faces. The raw reality of law enforcement can seriously do a number both your husband's and your own faith.

On shift, your husband sees some of the worst the world has to offer. On top of that, he sees them before they've been cleaned and sanitized for public viewing. He's the one who has to make sense of things before anybody else. He sees the raw emotions of those who've been wronged and the serious injuries humans can inflict on one another, even those they claim to love the most.

As a result, he often comes home broken and stressed out. As the person he loves most, you're unfortunately the person who usually bears the brunt of his emotional detachment or irritability. Sometimes he'll talk to you about what happened, but other times you just have to understand that you might never hear all the details of his day, even though the memory of whatever happened won't ever leave him.

The idea of being a woman who can laugh at the future seems extremely out there when even your day-to-day reality isn't all that laughable. The future feels completely unpredictable, even when it comes to whether you'll actually see your husband that day, or if he'll come home after you've already gone to bed. Add to that the danger he faces every single day, and the understanding that everything could change in a single moment, and you've got a situation that's hard on everyone.

On top of all that, he's painted as a criminal himself by most of the media. They say he's trigger-happy, power-hungry, and a danger to society, when the truth is so far from that. Those misconceptions mean he's in even more danger than ever before, and that makes you scared and angry for him since you know the truth of the matter. You know the man you're married to.

When everything in the world feels against you and your family, it can be hard to develop and sustain your faith in God. There is so much that works against that faith. It's hard to keep your head up in a world full of so much darkness, especially when people villainize those who fight the darkness.

I'd like to ask you a question, though: Have you ever thought that maybe there's a reason behind all of that?

Satan is ever present in this fallen world[26]. He doesn't look kindly on those who can be a force for good. When it comes to your husband and his calling as a police officer, he has a lot of potential to change the world for the better. It's no real wonder the enemy would target

---

[26] *1 Peter 5:8*

him for destruction. He doesn't like it, and will do everything he can to veer both of you off course.

When you recognize that Satan is always going to fight against the godly, those trials are easier to face. Your faith is easier to hang on to because you can understand that those are meant as a deterrent. You can swat them away like pesky flies rather than thinking they're meant by God to punish you.

Not only that, but God doesn't allow you to go through anything without a purpose. Satan might think he's powerful, but God is always infinitely more powerful. If He is allowing you to be tried and tested, know that it's not without merit. Heck, God allowed even Jesus to be tried and tested while on earth! No matter how much it hurts or how much it scares you, know that He is always good.

Even when life is scary and uncertain, you can have confidence that His plans are always good, always for the best, and that there is more to this life than we can see. You can laugh at the fear of the future knowing that even if the worst possible things happen, He will always be there to comfort you and to make it right.

This chapter is, in my mind, a culmination of the rest of the traits of the Proverbs 31 wife. Faith requires you to not only trust God, but also to serve Him. You can show your trust in Him through your humility and using your time in the way He asks you to. You can serve Him through comforting others and by choosing to live your life in a virtuous way.

Faith is behind all of these things, but all those things, in turn, serve to grow your faith. It sometimes feels like a chicken or the egg kind of thing, and that's true. Being a Proverbs 31 wife means constantly choosing good over evil in every aspect of your life, and doing so requires you to be spiritually-minded over temporally-minded. That requires the utmost faith in God.

This faith isn't a one-time decision you make to trust what He says and live accordingly. It's a lifelong process of trial and error; of testing, questioning, succeeding, failing, and seeing what the process is like. The overarching point of our entire lives is to learn to serve Him[27], which means our faithfulness will be tried and tested the entire time.

If you feel like you're not faithful enough for whatever reason, take heart. You don't need to have perfect faith to follow Him. Even if all you can do right now is *want* to have more faith in God, that's enough for Him to work with. Faith is always a process and He is no stranger to that. Even if you have doubts and questions right now, you can always choose to pursue Him in earnestness and He'll see you through any trial of faith.

This chapter is all about what having faith in God means, what you will receive by being faithful, and how to increase your confidence that He will always provide.

---

[27] *Revelation 4:11*

# SECTIONS

Finding the Opportunity In Every Crisis
God's Blessings
God Is Good Even When Life Isn't
Do What He Asks Of You

# FAITH
# FINDING THE OPPORTUNITY IN EVERY CRISIS

*And the God of all grace, who called you to his eternal glory in Christ, after you have suffered a little while, will himself restore you and make you strong, firm and steadfast.*
*1 Peter 5:10*

In early January this past year, I was feeling all out of sorts and decided to take a pregnancy test. I didn't actually think it would be positive. We hadn't been actively trying to get pregnant. I figured the "off-ness" was just a fluke, but almost immediately after I set the test on the counter, it came up positive. I'm pretty sure I literally gasped when I saw it, because I just couldn't believe it.

I couldn't contain myself. I laughed, cried, and jumped around the bathroom – and thank goodness I was alone at the time, because I think my son would have been a little freaked out by the outburst. When I called my husband to tell him the good news, he was just as excited. We'd wanted to have another baby for almost two years, so to see it actually happening was beyond exciting.

I felt like finally, after our long wait for baby #2 and all the trials we'd faced over those two years, God was smiling on us and was about to make everything right again. I prayed prayer after prayer of gratitude for the opportunity to have another baby. I took pleasure in every sign of sickness, even when I got a cold early in the pregnancy and could barely breathe. I was just so excited for the opportunity to expand our family.

About two months later, however, I started bleeding – badly. The day it started was an incredibly snowy Friday, so they told me to stay home unless it got worse. On Sunday, I went to church as usual, trying to stay positive. When I went to the bathroom midway through the service, I passed a huge clot. I knew it was time to go to the hospital, and I was absolutely terrified.

After waiting a few hours for the radiologist to see me (while my husband and I watched Cops, naturally, to take our mind off things), she wheeled me to the room with the ultrasound. She started the scan, and I got more and more nervous the longer she was silent. She smiled at me a little and told me she had to turn the screen for a second. She turned the screen away and began typing, but she hadn't turned it far enough. I watched as she typed the words I dreaded: no heartbeat.

I didn't want to admit I'd seen it. I didn't want to talk about it. Part of me didn't want to make her uncomfortable. Honestly, I hoped I could stop myself from even crying, but I couldn't. I turned my face away as tears silently began to stream down my face.

At 11 weeks pregnant, just shy of what I considered the "safe zone", just one week prior to the big announcement, one week before I could share all the good God had done for us, my precious baby was gone. I was crushed. Even two days later when I had to have a D&C, I remember sobbing as I went under sedation because I knew, for sure, I was about to not be pregnant anymore.

The whole heartbreaking time, however, I felt God's love more closely than ever. Even as we walked into the hospital that Sunday, I told my husband, "I don't think it's going to be good news, but I feel like it's going to be okay." Only God's love could have allowed me to have that peace in the face of such heartbreak. Through the next month, I regularly felt His comfort. Even when I felt like the whole situation was incredibly unfair, even when I was furious with God for allowing it to happen, I couldn't stop the nagging feeling that He'd allowed it to happen for a reason – whether I was supposed to know that reason or not.

Through the heartbreak, physical trauma, and financial strain the miscarriage caused, I tried to stay close to God because of the comfort He provided me right off the bat. I felt God assuring me that He wouldn't do anything that was not for my ultimate good. Through every moment of pain, I tried hard to see the silver linings – and honestly, there were a lot.

For one thing, because the miscarriage had been so expensive, we decided to get gung-ho about treatment for my husband's chronic pain. We figured if we were going to get so close to our out-of-pocket maximum and go into debt for something so unpleasant, why not spend a little more money to get him healthy? It's a long road, but we know it will be worth it so he can get back to the career he loves. Without the miscarriage, we wouldn't have felt so comfortable doing so.

Even though I would never necessarily celebrate having a miscarriage, looking back, I can confidently say that more good than bad has come out of the experience. Regardless of the pain I've gone through, I know God is forever on my side and working things for my good, even if I don't always understand it – just like the scripture at the beginning of this section states.

We all suffer in this life. Like Wesley says in the Princess Bride, "Life *is* pain, Highness. Anyone who says differently is selling something." Not a single one of us escape life unscathed. The difference between those who do so with joy and those who falter under the strain, then, comes down to where we choose to focus our attention.

When your husband comes home from a shift, goes straight to your room, sits on the bed and buries his face in his hands, remember that. When your husband refuses to talk to you about what terrible things he's seen and you struggle to know what to do to help, remember that. When you're facing the often ridiculous criticism of the anti-police crowd, remember that.

Whatever crisis you're facing right now, don't ever forget that God can make it work to your benefit. That's true no matter how severe or crushing the disappointment. You can always choose to find the opportunities in that crisis, because they will always, always be present.

If the crisis you're facing is a challenge to you or your husband's faith, you can use that challenge to strengthen your faith, or you can allow it to separate you from God. If you're facing difficulties in your marriage, you can use it to strengthen your marriage by recognizing what you need to work on and learning to speak more openly with your husband, or you can sit quietly and wait for things to fall apart. If you're struggling with self-doubt, you can either learn to give yourself grace, or quietly fall apart by yourself. If you're having a hard time with night shifts, you can choose to moan and groan about the loneliness, or you can use the alone time to better yourself.

The point is, when you're struggling, no matter what you're struggling with, make a point to be aware of the danger and instead choose the things that will allow you to take advantage of the opportunity. Either way, you have to make a choice. And in those choices lie your future: whether you're going to be better, or whether you're going to be worse. Whether you're going to succeed or fail. Whether you're going to be happy or miserable.

Take advantage of the opportunities you have, even if they present themselves as crises initially. Have faith that He sees everything that's going on, and choose to allow Him to work in you to change you for the better.

Remember that after you've struggled for a while, He will restore you to full glory. No matter how crushing the defeat, He won't allow it to be for nothing. It's just not how He works – so take a deep breath, dust yourself off, and keep on moving.

# PRAYER IDEAS

- Thank God for the promise that He will always work everything for your good.
- Thank God for always looking out for you, even when you can't understand what He's doing.
- Ask for help seeing the opportunity in whatever crisis you're currently facing.
- Ask for additional comfort until you understand His plan better.
- Ask for help determining your next steps when you feel like all is lost.

# FAITH
# GOD'S BLESSINGS

*Blessed are the poor in spirit,*
*for theirs is the kingdom of Heaven.*
*Matthew 5:3*

Tell me, honestly: Do you ever get the feeling everyone else has it way easier than you? If so, I can 100% relate. I've had that feeling many, many times over the past two years with our financial issues, strained family relationships and friendships with those we felt we were closest to, inability to have another baby, and my husband's increasingly poor physical health.

Even though I could find lots of silver linings in those challenges, it just didn't feel like enough. They felt more like consolation prizes than true blessings from God, especially when I looked at what was happening in the lives of others. I'll never forget the time we had friends over for dinner and one of them proclaimed how happy she was that life was finally falling into place for them. My husband and I were both completely silent.

Honestly, it's been so confusing, and I've questioned God in this process many, many times. Questions like: "Why doesn't He care about us?", "What am I doing wrong?", "How come everyone else gets the things I want?", "Am I not faithful enough?", "Does He even love us anymore?"

I was most confused because when we prayed about the things we wanted, it felt like He wanted us to have them, too. They seemed like things we should pursue, stuff that would make Him happy, too. I couldn't help but wonder why weren't we getting them if He wanted those things for us, too.

During that time of questioning, I received an answer that slowly took root in my heart, an answer I never actually expected – but one that has changed how I see everything.

It all began when I saw someone's social media post with the hashtags #blessed and #Godsigood. It rubbed me the wrong way, and I couldn't figure out why. It wasn't jealousy, per se. I mean, I know jealousy, and this wasn't it. It was just that something about it felt wrong. Incomplete. I mean, I've been annoyed by those things before, but I just couldn't get this one out of my head.

All day, I mulled it over, unsure why it was bugging me so much. Those kinds of posts have always annoyed me, but I never really took the time to consider why. That's when I came across the scripture at the beginning of this chapter: *blessed are the poor in spirit*. I'm sure I've heard that phrase thousands of times, but I never really stopped to think about it before.

When I thought about it, I started to understand. It wasn't this overwhelming, life-changing revelation, but one of those things where understanding began to slowly trickle in. The post wasn't bugging me because I was worried God wasn't being good to me. What bugged me was the realization that it failed to paint a complete picture of God. It didn't take into account that blessings aren't just stuff, and God isn't just good when life is good.

I'd never considered this idea at all before, and it was so big to me it honestly took a few days before I could fully digest it. There are so many scriptures that assure us that God only intends good for us. If He can't lie, that means He *always* keeps that promise, whether things actually look like blessings to us or not.

I realized I was making the same mistake as that original poster in thinking God wasn't being good to us just because superficially good things weren't happening. The reason I felt so bugged by those posts before was that they made me feel like God wasn't being good to me. Watching other people get what I wanted most made me feel like He was choosing not to bless me, when really, I'd been missing the point all along.

In reality, some of the most significant blessings God can offer us come through severe trials. True blessings from God aren't just Him giving us the desires of our heart. They're the things that will ultimately allow us to become more like Christ. They're the experiences that will bring us closer to Him. They're the heartbreaking moments that help us to mature. The disappointments and failures that hurt us the most are the ones that drive us to our knees seeking His comfort.

I've never understood this verse like I do now:

"Blessed are the poor in spirit, for theirs is the kingdom of heaven. Blessed are those who mourn, for they will be comforted. Blessed are the meek, for they will inherit the earth. Blessed are those who hunger and thirst for righteousness, for they will be filled. Blessed are the merciful, for they will be shown mercy. Blessed are those who are persecuted because of righteousness"[28]

---

[28] *Matthew 5:3-6, 10*

It doesn't say, "blessed are the prosperous." It doesn't say, "blessed are those who get everything they want." The blessed aren't those who never know trouble. This entire passage reminds us that the true blessings of God aren't always packaged in an obvious way. Only through seeking a deeper understanding of Him can we see them for what they are.

Your husband is a great example of someone who is persecuted because of righteousness, by the way. Seriously, Satan isn't a fan of law and order. He much prefers chaos and destruction. The fact that Satan actively mobilizes the people of the world against your husband is a sign that he's doing good things for God. Those things aren't a punishment from God for doing what He's asked of him (because evil doesn't come from Him). Your husband will not only be blessed and strengthened through the experience of law enforcement, but he'll also receive blessings in the life after this.

Likewise, because you're his partner in life, you'll bear part of that persecution, too. You might get it in less obvious ways, but you'll undoubtedly face a situation in which you feel in danger because of your husband's job. There are so many people out for blood when it comes to people who aren't even part of the police force, but simply support them.

It's hard and scary, but don't let that persecution break you down. Don't let it pull you away from God or dissuade you from doing the things He's asked you to do. If you can come to a true understanding of what His blessings look like, you can be brave in the face of uncertainty and, like the wife in Proverbs 31, be able to laugh at the future.

I know it's easy to get discouraged when you feel like everyone else is being blessed except for you. Trust me, I can relate. Whatever you're struggling with right now - whether it's police wife life in general, being a new mom, infertility, job loss, relationship difficulties, whatever – know that those struggles will be for your benefit. Know that they're happening for a reason, and God will see you through this trial.

Have faith that even if it doesn't feel like it now, you're going to get through this, and you will be stronger and better than ever before. God has never, and will never, let you down. That's not how He works, not even a little! So don't ever let that go. Stay strong, stay faithful, and keep moving forward.

# PRAYER IDEAS

- Thank God for the understanding that He is always working for your good, even when it may not feel like it.
- Thank God for understanding your shortcomings when it comes to having faith in what His blessings consist of.
- Thank God for always being there to comfort you during the hard times of life.
- Ask for help seeing the blessings in your struggles.
- Ask for help curbing feelings of envy when others get what you wish you could have.
- Ask for help in understanding His plan for you and having faith that He does have your long-term benefit in mind.

# FAITH
# KNOWING GOD IS GOOD EVEN WHEN LIFE IS NOT

*And we know that all things work together for good to them that love*
*God, to them who are the called according to his purpose.*
*Romans 8:28*

Before I actually became a police wife, I had some weirdly great preparatory experiences for the job. In college, I took a lot of classes on sexual violence and family violence. I wanted to work in the field, so I volunteered at a women's shelter after graduation. I've seen and heard a lot of things that made my husband's experiences not quite as shocking.

Side note: my knowledge of human trafficking and the sex industry made for an interesting class when my husband was in the academy. The teacher asked if anyone knew anything about prostitutes. My husband raised his hand, then immediately said something to the extent of, "No, it's not like that, it's because of my wife." Needless to say, he had some explaining to do. Oops.

In any case, even though I felt like I was totally prepared to back my husband when he faced horrors on the job, there are some things you just can't prepare yourself for. People do inexplicable, unimaginably awful things to one another, and that can be tough to wrap your mind around.

Even though my husband is pretty good at knowing what he can and can't share with me, he also sometimes doesn't realize how stories will affect me. Whether that's because he's already compartmentalized it or was simply unaware of something I'd experienced that day that made me more sensitive, it means that I've heard several stories I really didn't want to know about.

The whole thing is tough, because as much as you want to be there for your husband, it's hard on both of you when the stories affect you so deeply. The truth is, your husband faces a lot of terrible situations. It's understandable that you'd both be bugged by them. It doesn't mean you're weak or not cut out for being a police wife. It just means you're human.

That being said, sometimes knowing about all the wickedness in the world can do a number on your faith. When you know God to be perfect, always good, and all-powerful, sometimes you can't help but wonder why things had to happen the way they did. It results in something resembling the classic question: Why does God let bad things happen to good people?

On the surface, it doesn't make much sense. It seems like if He truly loved us, He would protect us from the bad things, because He can do anything. I don't blame you for occasionally wondering why He didn't stop something from happening. After all, we know we would want to keep bad things from happening to the people we love, right? If He loves us so perfectly, why would He allow bad things to happen to us?

It's hard enough to face this question when it's just about the mundane inconveniences of life, like being broke as a joke and subsisting on ramen. When the question concerns random, horrendous, senseless acts of violence, finding the answer to your questions is all the more important because it really is an understandable threat to your faith.

That being said, even though having a deeper understanding of the wickedness of the world can be a threat to your faith, it can also be the catalyst that builds your faith. That same knowledge that makes you question God can be the greatest asset you have in your journey of spiritual growth.

What it comes down to is never losing sight of one simple truth: God is always good.

Sometimes the terrible stories you hear about make you feel like God is, at best, indifferent, and at worst, just plain mean. For instance, children orphaned because someone else chose to drive drunk? The abusive husband who finagles a way to keep control of the household finances, house, cars, and all other assets, while the wife is left destitute, trying to rebuild her life as a single mom? How is that fair?

No matter what the case may be, the fact remains that God is never indifferent and never mean. If He were, He would cease to be God. God is love, and we are His children. He feels just as heartbroken as we do for the pain we have to go through, but His ways aren't our ways. His timing isn't our timing, and His plans are not our plans. He sees beyond what we can in this mortal existence, and knows that everything can serve a purpose for good.

Remember that in His goodness, He is also powerful. None of the pain and ugliness we see in this world is greater than Him. No bad thing is beyond His ability to make it right. He has the power to turn your greatest failure into the launchpad for your greatest success. He can turn anything your enemies intend for evil into a force for your good.

When you think about it, His power is made even more beautiful in the messy situations of life. The powerful good that can come from unspeakable evil is astounding at times. It's something that could only be done by a perfectly loving, all-knowing being. When you think of it that way, your faith can be built, layer upon layer.

When you find yourself doubting God's goodness, remember that you can always talk to Him about it. He is big enough to handle any and every question that comes His way, as long as you ask in the right spirit. He'll always be there for you whether you're hurting because of something you've experienced or something you're suffering secondhand. If you seek Him, you will undoubtedly find Him[29].

In my experience, every time I've turned to God with my questions, I've received an answer. Sometimes I receive the answer that what the person was faced with was meant to make them stronger, even if it hurts in the meantime. Sometimes, the answer is simply that humans are blessed with the power to make their own choices – and when those choices hurt others, God can and will make it right when the time comes. Sometimes, the question is answered with a question: *do you believe there's more to this life?* Which means to me that there's more beyond this world. That whether things are made right in this life doesn't necessarily matter, even if that's what I feel *should* happen.

Whatever the answer is, however it comes, it's always accompanied by a sense of peace. After all, He isn't annoyed by the fact we feel heartbroken for those around us. He wants us to love others, to want to lift them up, and to come to Him for help doing so. When we're feeling hurt or confused, He's happy to help us when we turn to Him.

When you're faced with terrible situations, you also need to remember that Christ overcame the world for you. Those terrible things your husband sees? They mean you have a better idea of what Christ

---

[29] *Jeremiah 29:13*

actually paid for on the cross. Knowing the depths of human sorrow can bring you closer to Him, because you know the enormity of the sacrifice He made. Because of your experiences as a police wife, you know better than the average person the weight of the sins He had to bear, the vast number of things He had to atone for. That's incredible, right?

If you can use the terrible things you hear to build your faith instead of break it, you've assisted God in using that awfulness as a force for good. You can be the first step in the good outcomes of bad situations, and that's kind of awesome.

No matter what awful thing you hear that weighs on your heart, know that God is always going to be there to help you make sense of it. Never doubt that He is still good, even when the things you see in the world around you aren't.

# PRAYER IDEAS

- Thank God for the assurance that He is a perfectly good, loving God, no matter what the people of the world choose to do.
- Thank God for the opportunity to understand Him better through the wickedness of the world.
- Ask for help understanding your deepest spiritual questions, knowing He will always respond.
- Ask for comfort when the evil you see brings you down.
- Ask for help comforting your husband when the world brings him down.

# FAITH
# DO WHAT HE ASKS OF YOU

*Walk in obedience to all that the Lord your God has commanded you, so that you may live and prosper and prolong your days in the land that you will possess.*
*Deuteronomy 5:33*

When my husband and I have lazy nights together in bed, one of our favorite things to watch is Live PD. He loves having the opportunity to see what's happening in real time with other police departments, and I enjoy being able to ask him questions about what's going on. Plus, it's easy to follow the story line even if we're working on other stuff while we watch it.

There's one thing that comes up almost every single time on Live PD, though, that I imagine has got to be the most frustrating thing ever for police officers. It's that people *do not listen* to what the officers are telling them to do. Sometimes I have to laugh, because their attitude and disobedience to lawful commands gets them in way more trouble than if they'd just quiet down and do what the officer asks.

It's so darn simple! You'd think at some point, people, especially the repeat offenders, would get the point that simply cooperating is the best way to leave the situation with the least amount of trouble.

Yet, time and time again you see people choosing not to cooperate — then complaining when they get arrested or tased, whatever the case may be.

The thing they don't recognize is that the officers aren't there with the intention of making their lives miserable. They're there to do a job. If the perpetrators would choose to show the officers respect, it would be smooth sailing. They might still get a ticket or court date or whatever else as a result of their actions, but at least they wouldn't get hit with additional charges. Everyone would come out of the situation happier.

When I think of being obedient (as in the opening verse of this chapter), that's one of the first things that comes to mind. While it's definitely not a perfect comparison, there are a few commonalities in the interaction of perpetrator and police officer and us and our Father in Heaven.

Like your officer in that situation, God has the authority to tell you what to do. Obviously He has much greater authority than any police officer, but bear with me. He created you. He gave you life. That gift in and of itself means you owe it to Him to do the best you can to do the things He asks.

Not only does God have authority to tell you what to do, He also has your best interest in mind. He wants good things for you. He wants to give you all the chances in the world, because He wants you to come back to Him. However, He isn't willing to tolerate disrespect or disobedience. He knows what's best for us, and if we choose not to do it, there will always be consequences — whether that means going down a path we shouldn't necessarily have gone down and dealing with the thorns along the way, or having to swallow our pride and repent of serious wrongdoings.

I got to thinking about the importance of being obedient to God about the time my son turned three. He seemed to skip right over the classic "terrible twos" stage and I foolishly thought I'd lucked out. When he turned three, woah. Different story. It was all fits, screaming, hitting, and generally refusing to listen.

I had a tough time understanding how to handle him. I wanted to be gentle and understanding, but when he hit me and screamed in my face, gentleness didn't come all that easily. There was a lot of putting him in his room and slamming the door because I couldn't have him near me. He knew how to press all the right buttons to make me so angry I felt I could hardly see straight.

One night, I prayed about how to parent him in a godly way, and in the way he needs to be parented. The next day, after he had calmed down from one of his tantrums, I sat down next to him on his bed and talked to him. The phrase that immediately came to mind was, "Mommy and Daddy want to keep you happy and safe. If you do what we ask you to do, you'll stay happy and safe."

When the phrase came out of my mouth, it kind of made me pause. It was completely an answer to my prayer to parent in a more God-like manner. I had never thought about God that way before, but the more I considered it, the more it made complete sense to use this phrase with our son. It's exactly how our Heavenly Father parents us.

Just like we tell our toddler things to keep him happy and safe (like, if you stand on your truck it'll break and you'll be sad, or if you run into the street you're going to get hurt), your Heavenly Father also wants to keep us happy and safe. Because of that, He also tells us what we should and shouldn't do.

Just like with my toddler and me, though, it's not always easy to do what He says. We don't have the same perspective as God. We can't see the totality of everyone's circumstances in relation to our own, so being obedient is a huge act of faith. We have to jump without actually knowing the outcome, trusting that He has things all planned out and that He is working things in our favor.

Obviously, there are a few basic things God asks everyone to do, like the ten commandments. Those are pretty obvious in how they'll keep us happy and safe – they allow us to avoid temptation and avoid the heartbreak that comes from betraying those around us through things like adultery. Those have their difficulties, but they're the simplest ones, in my opinion.

Where it gets sticky is when God asks us to do things on an individual level, things that are specifically for us to do. Doing so requires a greater amount of faith, trust, and humility, and God often uses these experiences to help build those things – which means He asks stuff that's initially outside of your comfort zone. That's the only way He can help you grow, after all!

When you pray about everything, you're bound to get answers that sometimes don't make a lot of sense to you. For me, it reminds me a lot of that part in Harry Potter where he takes the luck potion, and suddenly wants to go to Hagrid's hut, saying, "I just feel like it's the place to be right now," and from there on out things all go exactly as he wants – but not in the way he or any of his friends would have expected.

God's plans are pretty similar most of the time. He might ask you to do things that don't make a lot of sense, but if you get an answer to a prayer that doesn't make sense to you, all you need to do is ask for confirmation. If you get the sense that's really what He wants you to do, do it, knowing that He'll never steer you wrong. It's not His way of doing things.

The more often you do this, the more you'll be able to feel Him leading and guiding you. When you seek His guidance with a humble spirit, having faith in the fact He loves you and wants you to be happy and safe, He can perform miracles. He can help open the floodgates of Heaven and let good stuff rain down on the heads of you and those around you.

When God asks you to do something, how willing are you to follow His guidance? It might depend on what we're talking about, really. I personally tend to have an easier time doing what He says when it comes to big things rather than little things. The big things seem somewhat more obvious and important, but the little things – like when I feel like I should stop and say something nice to someone, even though I'm in the middle of juggling a bunch of groceries and/or a grumpy toddler? It's easier to brush off those impressions.

However, having faith in God means allowing Him to be in the driver's seat. It means acknowledging that His thoughts are higher than yours, and thus His plans are way better thought out than you could ever dream. If you trust Him, you can rely on the fact that if you subvert your own plans for His, you can be assured that He'll always make things work for your good.

Let God guide you. Be receptive to His promptings and pray to know if there's anything more you can do, let him open your eyes to anything you've neglected to pay attention to thus far. Pray to have a softened heart that's receptive to His promptings and help you to recognize them and have the discernment to recognize them for what they are.

# PRAYER IDEAS

- Thank God for knowing what you need most and guiding you to make those things happen.
- Thank God for his ability to help you be happier and safer, physically and spiritually.
- Pray to be more sensitive to His promptings, and the discernment necessary to know what comes from Him and what comes from your own thoughts or other outside influences.
- Pray for help in being more obedient to what He asks you to do.
- Pray for greater faith in His plan for your life and that of your loved ones.
- Ask for help making the right decisions in everyday situations.

# FINAL THOUGHTS

*Honor her for all that her hands have done,*
*and let her works bring her praise at the city gate.*
*Proverbs 31:31*

At the close of this devotional, I want to encourage you to remember a few things.

First of all, remember that improving any of your habits is going to take time. In fact, the original section of Proverbs 31 that talks about the wife of noble character is written as an acrostic poem, where each verse begins with the successive letter of the Hebrew alphabet. It was designed to be something people could easily remember that would help you improve over time. It was never meant as a read-once-and-implement-everything type thing in the first place.

Know that you won't learn everything you need to know in a day or two. You can't be transformed over the course of a single devotional. It takes consistent effort over time to become more like Him. Don't worry about feeling like you're not enough right now. That's not what matters most. What truly matters to Him is your constant forward progress.

Instead of beating yourself up for not being who you want to be, prayerfully consider what trait (or traits) of the Proverbs 31 wife you should focus on right now. It might be obvious for some people, but maybe for you it's not. That's okay! Trust that if you ask, He will always guide you to what you need to know. He will always look kindly on your desire to become better through His guidance.

Remember that He will always be there to help you on your journey. When you're feeling weak, let Him be your strength. When you're feeling angry or sad or scared, talk to Him about it. Let Him help you carry your emotional load. It's what He's there for. Don't ever think He has left you on your own, because He's already promised He never will[30]. Hold tight to that promise in all that you do.

Keep in mind that having faith in that promise will become easier as you develop a closer relationship with your Heavenly Father over time. Like any relationship, though, it's something that has to be slowly built: day by day, small effort by small effort. Doing the things detailed in this devotional is a great way to help you deepen your relationship with Him, but go wherever the Spirit takes you. Your relationship with Him is a completely personal matter, and it's between you and Him to know what matters most for you.

Remember that, in everything you do, mistakes will always be part of the process. Mistakes are some of the greatest teachers. God knows that. If you look at them that way, too, you can feel free to give yourself a little more grace than you might otherwise. Know that in every mistake you make, He will always be there to help pick you up, dust you off, dry your tears, and help you make things right again.

Finally, remember that you will always be a daughter of God. No matter what changes happen in your life, no matter what trials or persecution you face, no matter what gigantic mistakes you make, no

---

[30] *Deuteronomy 31:6*

matter what tragedies happen to you, that will never change. He will always love you, no matter what happens. Even if you stray, He will always want you. He will always welcome the repentant sinner home with open arms.

Becoming closer to God and doing the things He most wants you to do will help you become the wife, mother, sister, daughter, and woman you've always wanted to be. As you develop your relationship with Him, you will learn to be the woman who is clothed in strength and dignity. You will have the faith necessary to laugh at the future, no matter how bleak things look at times in the field of law enforcement. You will have the strength to do all that He asks of you, all the things those around you need you to do, without feeling unduly overwhelmed.

The thing I most want you to take away from this book is that you can always feel confident knowing everything is in His hands. No matter where you are in this moment, you are exactly where you need to be for your good and for His glory. Nothing happens that He doesn't know about.

If you continue to focus on staying close to God at all times and seeking Him through every blessing and trial, you will undoubtedly stand victorious at the end of this life. Everything will work together for the good of those who love God, and by doing the things that bring you closer to Him, you can express that love more fully.

All these things will bring you and your husband honor, even if not in this life, in the life to come. Continue to build your treasure in heaven so that no matter what the world can throw at you and your husband, you can withstand it. Be strong in your faith, knowing that no weapon formed against you shall prosper[31], even if those weapons look scary sometimes.

---

[31] *Isaiah 54:17*

Most of all, remember to keep on going no matter what happens. Don't let anyone or anything drag you down. Choose to press forward with faith in Christ, regardless of what anyone else does. The choice is on you, and when you understand all that God promises you in return, the choice is simple.

I want you to know: you've got this! God will never let you down, so take heart as you press forward and do the things He needs you to do. You can be a force for good, both in your family and in the world. He needs you to be His hands and feet, so go — be His hands and feet and make this world a better place, one small faithful decision at a time. ❤

# ACKNOWLEDGEMENTS

I have so many people to thank for helping me complete this book, I don't even know where to start!

I suppose I could start with my editor, Erin. This devotional would have been kind of a wreck without her honesty – and recognition of some pretty funny mistakes. She helped me turn the words I wrote into what I was actually trying to say. Seriously, you're worth your weight in gold (or maybe you need to pack on a few pounds, I'm not sure).

Of course, my husband has been invaluable in the process, too, in the form of a shoulder to cry on, someone to provide me with napping opportunities when possible, an encouragement to keep going when I got scared and wanted to quit, and the ultimate recognizer of me getting overly stressed and doing what he could to help me. I love you with all my heart!

I also had many friends take my son when I was feeling overwhelmed with writing and editing work (and momming in general). I so appreciate you taking the time out of your busy schedules to entertain my kiddo for a few hours! Hopefully he didn't wear you out too much.

I'd also like to thank all the bloggers I've met through Elite Blog Academy and the Activate conference. You guys have encouraged me time and time again not to give up when things are hard, and I can't thank you enough for all the support you've given me over the years! Honestly, there are too many in that group to name — but you know who you are. I couldn't have done any of this without being able to share the good times and bad times with you!

Oh, and have I mentioned my launch team? Seriously, the ladies who helped me get this book off the ground have been amazing. They reached out to lots of bloggers and podcasters who I never would have reached out to myself (especially podcasters, because — well, there's a reason I write, not talk. I'm awkward.) Thank you for helping spread the word about my book, and push myself outside of my comfort zone to do so!

Also, small shoutout to the officer in the section about progress over perfection — the ticket is officially paid, and I don't begrudge you one bit. Thanks for being so nice!

Seriously, there are endless people who have encouraged me throughout this process, and I'm so grateful for every single one of you. You've made such a difference in my life, and I absolutely can't thank you enough!

Oh — and you, reader! If it wasn't for you, none of this would be possible (or, I guess necessary). Thank you so much for your support, and I hope I've been able to help you through this devotional.

I'm so excited to be able to share my writing with the world, and I'm beyond grateful for everyone who made it happen.

# ABOUT THE AUTHOR

Leah Everly is the blogger behind Love and Blues Blog, where she helps police wives in their often difficult calling. When she's not busy writing, she can usually be found wrangling her toddler or snuggled up with her nose in a book. She lives in Salt Lake City with her husband, a former police officer, and their son, who will be joined in a few short months by a baby girl.

If you'd like to follow more of Leah's writings, check her out on loveandbluesblog.com.

# COULD YOU DO ME A QUICK FAVOR?

Hi there — Leah here :)

I hope you've enjoyed this devotional!

If that's been the case, would you mind leaving a review of the book on Amazon? It would be a HUGE help to me in getting this book in the hands of those who need it most.

Thank you so much, and have an awesome day!

Love,
Leah

Made in the USA
Middletown, DE
04 June 2020